The Paradigm Pastor

Jesus as a Paradigm
for the
Pastor of Today

TRUDY U. PETTIBONE

© 2014

Published in the United States by Nurturing Faith Inc., Macon GA, www.nurturingfaith.net.

Library of Congress Cataloging-in-Publication Data is available.

978-1-938514-58-6

All rights reserved. Printed in the United States of America

About the Cover
The recorded insights of Roman philosopher Cicero (106 BC - 43 BC) helped form the core of the well-known saying: "The eyes are the window to the soul." This cover attempts a glimpse of the life, ministry and person of Jesus through a focus on the eyes of an unknown Sicilian artist's mosaic. The mosaic's multiple colors also reflect the many layers to Jesus and his ministry.

Cover design by Amy C. Cook. Illustration courtesy of istockphoto.com.
Mosaic: Christ's Face. (Credit: Fausto Renda, istockphoto.com)

Contents

Introduction..vii

PART ONE: ASPECTS OF THE PASTORATE IN JESUS' LIFE

1. Jesus as Preacher..3
   (Matthew 5–7)

2. Jesus as Teacher..11
   (Matthew 10; John 7:14-24; Mark 2:13; Mark 6:30)

3. Jesus as Shepherd...17
   (Mark 10:35-40; Matthew 16:21-24; John 13:5-10;
   10:11-14, 27; 14:26; 18:10-11)

4. Jesus as Evangelist..21
   (Matthew 4:17, 23; 6:33; 10:7; Mark 10:14; Parables)

5. Jesus as Enabler/Preparer...25
   (John 21:15-25; 14:12; 20:21-22; Luke 10:1-11; 24:49)

6. Jesus as Caregiver..29
   (Mark 1:30-31; John 19:26-27)

7. Jesus as Sacrificer and Sacrifice..33
   (John 10:15; 2 Corinthians 5:21;
   1 Peter 2:24; Hebrews 2:17)

8. Jesus as Social Activist...37
   (Luke 7:11-16; Matthew 14:15-21)

9. Jesus as Tradition Breaker..41
   (Matthew 15:1-20; 5:17)

10. Jesus as Embracer..45
    (Matthew 19:13-14; 9:9-12; Luke 19:2-9)

11. Jesus as Intercessor..49
    (John 17)

12. Jesus as Servant...53
    (John 13)

13. Jesus as Organizer..57
    (Matthew 10:1-16; Luke 6:13; John 15:16)

Part Two: Jesus as Example of His Teachings

1. Love..65
   (Mark 12:30-31; John 13:34; 14:21; 15:9)

2. Obedience...69
   (John 12:49; 14:15)

3. Childlike Faith...71
   (Mark 10:15)

4. Servanthood..75
   (John 5:36)

Part 3: Other Pastoral Factors of Jesus' Ministry

1. Congregations..81
   (Luke 9:18; Matthew 4:25)

2. Outsiders...85
   (Matthew 15:22-28; 8:5-10)

3. Detractors..89
   (Matthew 9:34; 22:23-33; Mark 3:22)

4. Pastor Killers...93
   (Mark 10:33; 14:64)

5. Devoted Followers..97
   (Matthew 27:55-56; Mark 16:1, 9; Luke 10:39, 42;
   John 20:11-17; 11:1-45; 12:1-8)

6. Preparation..103
   (Luke 2:41-52; Matthew 3:13-17; 4:1-11)

7. Provision...109
   (Matthew 27:55; Mark 15:40-41;
   Luke 8:3; 2 Chronicles 31:5-9)

8. Aftermath..113
   (John 20:11-28; 21:15-24; Acts 1:6-11; 2)

Introduction

I never planned to be a pastor. Others saw the possibility in my life, but it was never on my horizon. Only as I was compelled to preach while I served in an associate position did I realize that I would never be happy doing anything that did not involve preaching—or at least sermon preparation.

Once it was clear that the Lord was leading me in the direction of the pastorate, I began to consider what my ministry would involve. I was blessed to begin pastoral ministry in an interim position, with a church that exercised reverse pastoral care and cared greatly for me. The eighteen months I spent in that place was a good foundation, but it never could have prepared me for what was to come.

Following six years pastoring a two-church parish, I was called to serve a church where the potential for ministry seemed boundless. This church, unlike the first in which I served, considered the pastorate as a secondary position within the church, under the leadership of either a Unified Board or the Moderator. Although I faced frustration in this position, I also had the joy of seeing a handful of people growing in faith and their walk with the Lord. Through it all, I always tried to remember the example of the One who, in my mind, exemplifies the pastorate, although we rarely use the term "Pastor" to describe Jesus.

As we look at Jesus' ministry, we can see all the elements of the pastorate: teaching, preaching, pastoral care, training, and frustration, to name a few. Jesus had devoted followers and detractors, even pastor killers, as he trained twelve men to do ministry after him. Of course, many of the terms we use metaphorically, Jesus knew literally. Jesus probably had the greatest "ministry of preparation" that ever existed. His ministry was supported, so he did not have to try to earn his subsistence as he ministered. To the extent that no other could do, he sacrificed himself for the people he served.

Not only did Jesus' ministry have all the elements of the pastorate, but he was an example of everything he taught. We will look at a few of the many aspects of Jesus' life in which he was an example of all that he taught.

Finally, besides what Jesus did, we will look at other occurrences in his life that match situations and events in the modern pastorate. There are very few ways, if any, in which we can look at Jesus' life and not see some picture of the pastorate. Jesus is model and paradigm for every pastor who wants to be what the Lord has called and prepared him or her to be.

Part One

Aspects of the Pastorate in Jesus' Life

While Jesus was the exemplary pastor, this was, of course, not his main mission. Jesus came to reconcile all creation with its Creator, and, in the process, provided forgiveness of sin and salvation to all those who would receive it. This is why we serve Jesus, but looking at his life through the lens of the pastorate can, I believe, provide a much better understanding of this challenging and rewarding position.

There are many texts that support each element of the pastorate that we will examine in Jesus' life, but I have chosen a few for each one. Hopefully, these will give us a good look into each aspect of Jesus' pastoral ministry.

1

Jesus as Preacher

Matthew 5-7

> *Luke 4:18*
> *"The Spirit of the Lord is on me, because he has anointed me to preach good news to the poor. He has sent me to proclaim freedom for the prisoners and recovery of sight for the blind, to release the oppressed, to proclaim the year of the Lord's favor."*

Abraham Lincoln once said, "I don't like to hear cut, canned, dried sermons. When I hear a man preach, I like to see him act like he was fighting bees."[1]

I tend to think that, while Jesus may not have looked like someone fighting bees, his sermons were never canned or dried. The exemplar of Jesus' preaching ministry is, I believe, the Sermon on the Mount, found in Matthew 5–7. These challenging words must have come at the congregation like a barrage of bees—sometimes stinging, sometimes just annoying, but always to the point.

According to Matthew 5:1, Jesus was above the

people, on a mountain, while the people might have been on a plain. Mark 6:17 says that Jesus came down with his disciples to a "level place." This is like the difference between preaching from a raised lectern and preaching from the floor of the sanctuary. Being on the same level as the people creates a much better sense of intimacy. Equal placement might have better captured the attention of people who were not used to being preached at from a raised platform. Some, however, were accustomed to the structure of the synagogues and might not have been so inclined to listen to someone who was right at their level.

The Sermon on the Mount—or plain—begins with nine blessings that we call the Beatitudes. Some pastors like to start a message with a humorous anecdote to get the attention of their audiences; others like to get into the message without an introduction. Jesus chose to startle his congregation, using an effective "waker-upper." If anyone were tempted to sleep through this sermon, they would have been hard pressed to do so.

Jesus started out by saying that the poor in spirit are members of the "kingdom of heaven" (Matt 5:3). This countercultural statement would certainly have gotten the attention of the religious leaders. In their view, God's kingdom was for the pious, the righteous, the wealthy, and the powerful, not those who might, for various reasons, have been on the cusps of society and rejected by those who saw themselves as righteous before God.

Then, after proclaiming the comfort of those who mourn, Jesus said that the meek would inherit the earth. Again, any Pharisees, Sadducees, or scribes who might have been present probably sputtered and spattered as they tried to comprehend these radical words.

Jesus began this lengthy sermon with promises that would have made the common person in the congregation finally feel as if they amounted to something. They knew persecution and could appreciate the promise of a heavenly reward. If they were humble, peaceable, and without guile, Jesus' words brought a sense of well-being that many had probably never known before.

It is often difficult to preach to a congregation of both believers and nonbelievers, people who walk strongly in the faith and people who are barely surviving spiritually. Throughout this sermon, Jesus bridges the gap beautifully.

I used to close my benedictions by encouraging the people to "go forth, being salt and light." I did this for some time, making one of those dangerous assumptions of understanding, before I actually preached on the meaning of those terms, perhaps from this text (Matt 5:13-16). After that sermon, someone came up to me and said, "Now I know what you mean by salt and light." As Jesus encouraged the people to be salt and light, they likely had a better understanding of those terms than we might have. Even though Jesus often preached in parables, he used ordinary terms that everyone could relate to, whether or not they fully understood the meaning of the parable.

This sermon consists of a chain of series. After saying that he had come to fulfill the law rather than to abolish it (Matt 5:17-20), Jesus sets out to alter the law with a series of "You have heard" statements. The law Jesus is altering is not the Law of Moses but the man-made law that has developed over the centuries between Moses' time and Jesus' time.

In each of these six statements, Jesus reminds the people of what they should be aware of, and then he gives a "new way." Jesus preaches with great authority. I don't know how many preachers can say, "But I say to you," "Do such and such," or that "such and such" should be the case and have the confidence that their listeners will comply and accept their teachings. These "you have heard" statements would have shocked both the religious establishment and the common people. In his preaching, Jesus was an equal-opportunity disturber.

Jesus changes form after the first two "you have heard" statements by saying, "It was also said." Like his location on the people's level, this variety helps keep their attention. We don't know that Jesus ever formally studied homiletics, but he could teach them in many quarters.

Jesus tells the people that murder is no longer just the actual taking of a life; it is also anger with a member of your family, whether it is the family of blood or the family of faith. That would have gotten my attention. Who hasn't had overwhelming thoughts of anger toward a family member?

Jesus changed adultery from a physical act to a hidden thought. How many people listening to him would have thought that he was preaching directly to them, that somehow he had gotten an inside track to their heart? A truly effective preacher will strike home with many. Some will respond with repentance and others with anger, and it seems certain that Jesus elicited both responses.

In these six "you have heard" statements, Jesus goes from saying that anger is a form of murder to advising the love of enemies and prayers for persecutors. This is the opposite of expectations, even today, and is a revolutionary idea. I had an experience where a couple in the parish I served became my enemies. I prayed diligently in this situation, not so much that they would change, but that I might trust the Lord for my responses to them. The way the Lord worked through that situation is amazing. Had I, as the pastor, not followed Jesus' instruction, my ministry would have been seriously harmed.

In the beginning of Matthew 6, we see an interlude in the chain of series. Jesus talks to the people about their attitude in giving, praying, and fasting. While he will later specifically name groups of people who carry out the behaviors he is describing, at this point he speaks of them anonymously. It is likely, however, that his listeners knew exactly who he was talking about.

As he speaks of praying, Jesus does something that, again, I think few pastors would do. He creates a new paradigm. We call his words, in verses 9 through 13, the Lord's Prayer or the model prayer. What contemporary pastor would include in his sermon a whole new format for praying? In a Bible study on prayer, I might encourage the participants to consider new ways to pray, but this seems unlikely during a sermon. Unfortunately, this model prayer has become a standard part of many services, sometimes losing its beauty and meaning in modern congregations. We need to restore the intent of Jesus and study how we can use this model for other prayers.

The next series of Jesus' sermon are the "do not" statements, beginning at 6:19. These are actual imperatives, commands, given by Jesus. I don't know if I have ever commanded a congregation to do something, but of course I do not carry the authority that Jesus had. It is amazing, so early in his ministry, that the people actually imparted such authority to him. True authority is not assumed; it is received from the people over whom the authority is exercised. Jesus preached with the authority of being the Son of God, but he also seems to have received the acceptance of that authority from the people. This is a good thing for a pastor.

Ironically, Jesus ends this series of negative "do not" commands with a brief series of positive commands. Again, this variety in form helps to keep the attention of the audience. The words weren't bad, either: "ask and it will be given; knock and the door will be opened; seek and you will find." These are wonderful promises that must have lifted the hearts of those who lived in hopelessness and oppression.

The end of these positive commands is what has come to be called the Golden Rule: do unto others as you would have them do unto you. Don't we all, as pastors, wish that our words would have as lasting an impact as many of Jesus' words?

Finally, at the end of this sermon, the last of the chain, Jesus gives a series of warnings. While many of the things he has spoken of have practical applications, Jesus now ventures more into the spiritual. I think that is a good way to structure a sermon: going from the physical/material to the spiritual.

I wonder how many people understood what he said when he told them to "enter through the narrow gate." Did people know that he was talking about eternal life? Was that concept well ingrained in their hearts? How did they feel when they heard Jesus say that the road to life is hard and few find it?

A lot of people today don't want to hear this kind of preaching because it is exclusionary. Jesus didn't seem worried about being exclusionary. He spoke the truth, which was that many will make it into the kingdom, but the majority will not.

Much of Jesus' preaching, such as the above example, would not be welcome in many churches today. I once included the words of 7:21-23 in a message, and I was later accused of being manipulative. How dare we say that some people who work all their lives for the church will not be accepted into the kingdom when their time on this earth ends? Well, Jesus dared to say this, and, if we are going to follow his model, we also must dare to say it.

I love the way the narrator describes the end of the sermon (7:28-29). We are told that the crowds were astounded. Does that seem like an understatement? Along with their astonishment, I believe the lives of many were changed. That is the goal of faithful preaching: to bring people into the kingdom of God so that their lives might be changed by the Presence of that same God.

I have mentioned Jesus' authority throughout this chapter, but the narrator gives us something to compare it with. Jesus "taught as one having authority, and not as their scribes." Imagine being in a church where there is no pastoral authority, where the preacher isn't familiar with the scriptural texts and often focuses more on personal agenda than on the Source. The scribes of Jesus' day were educated—they might be equivalent to our lawyers—but they were like many of the professors I had in my college and graduate courses. They knew the texts and they knew the words, but somehow they missed the meaning and the significance that flows through the text. They taught the text from a natural intellectual or cognitive perspective rather than from a spiritual perspective. First Corinthians 2:14 tells us that the unspiritual are not able to understand the things of God's Spirit. Scripture is a spiritual undertaking, breathed by God's Spirit into those who wrote and redacted the texts (2 Tim 3:16). Without the help of the Spirit for understanding, the texts of Scripture are just words.

To those who have the ability to understand them, they are life and strength. The scribes of Jesus' day did not have the spiritual means to teach the texts authoritatively.

Twice in this text (5:19 and 7:28), we see a reference to Jesus' teaching. Any good sermon, of course, should have an educational element to it. While this "Sermon on the Mount" has the definite tone of a sermon, it consists heavily of teaching elements. In 1 Timothy 5:17, Paul refers to the elders who "labor in preaching and teaching." These two gifts—preaching and teaching—are so closely related that we don't know if Paul intends them as one or two gifts within the church. So as we now look at Jesus as Teacher, we might find that what we identify as teaching seems like preaching. In either case, people are listening, entering the kingdom and having their lives changed by the power of God, all of which should be the goal of every pastor.

Reflection Questions

What aspects of Jesus' preaching do you follow in your ministry?

Does your preaching always proclaim the Kingdom of God?

Note

[1] "Preaching," in *1001 More Humorous Illustrations*, ed. Michael Hodgin (Grand Rapids MI: Zondervan, 1998), 259.

2

Jesus as Teacher

Matthew 10; John 7:14-24;
Mark 2:13; Mark 6:30

> *Timothy 4:11*
> *Command and teach these things.*

One of the best teaching experiences I've had was teaching a Sunday school class of sixth grade girls. And one of the best series of lessons we had, which extended to two quarters, was on the book of Revelation. Looking back on that experience, conducted during the early days of my walk with the Lord, I wonder how effective I was. What did I really know? What did those girls learn? I certainly never thought of myself as having any authority.

During the approximately three years of Jesus' "official" ministry on earth, he taught prodigiously, and while he was often surrounded by the masses, the focus of most of his teaching was a group of twelve men. We call them his disciples, a word that has the meaning of "pupil" or follower. These twelve, coming from various walks of life, were brought under the tutelage of one of the greatest teachers of all time. Jesus taught with knowledge, authority, wisdom, and compassion, and he conveyed these qualities to his pupils. That should be the goal of every teacher: to prepare pupils to meet the challenges of their life to come.

In Matthew 10, we see the most precise description of Jesus' preparation of his disciples. The first thing we are told is that Jesus conveyed authority over evil to them. These men had seen Jesus minister to others, exercising that same authority, and now it was time for them to begin their internship in ministry. Jesus didn't keep the students in the classroom. He sent them out with specific instructions. He told them the auspices under which they would minister: they were going out into a world of wolves, so they were to be wise as serpents but innocent as doves (10:16). If they were apprehended on account of their ministry, they were not to be concerned with defending themselves, because the Spirit would provide what they needed at the time (10:19-20). Jesus warned them of persecution to come, persecution that would happen because they were his disciples.

Jesus did not try to paint an unrealistically rosy picture for these disciples. He told them what they were to proclaim, and he explained the dangers of that proclamation. Jesus taught them that following him would cost them dearly. Their lives must be grounded in him, and, even if they lost it all, they would find life.

One excellent teaching method that Jesus employed was feedback. Mark 6:30 tells us that the disciples shared with Jesus their experiences of field ministry. Jesus had sent them out two by two, and it is not hard to imagine their excitement as they came back to him and discussed their mission. I wonder if he gave advice as to what they should or should not have done. Just giving them the opportunity to discuss their experiences with him was invaluable. Even when Jesus hasn't sent them out, we see him following up on discussions that they've had among themselves (e.g., Mark 2:8). It was important to Jesus that his followers had true and proper understanding, and he was not afraid to challenge them in areas they should not have been discussing.

I wonder what these fishermen, tax collectors, and others felt about being pupils of Jesus by the time he finished this stage of their preparation. One eventually turned away, but none turned back to their former lives for any significant length of time. After the crucifixion, Peter returned to fishing, but he soon learned that he would permanently be engaged in another profession. As a teacher, Jesus perfectly fulfilled the "ministry of preparation" to which all teachers are called. After Pentecost, these who had sat at the feet of Jesus demonstrated that they had been taught well, because they learned well.

Pastors of churches have the beautiful responsibility of preparing people for ministry. It is rewarding to see people commit their lives to the Lord, and then to help them understand what sharing that life with others will entail. Some churches make it their ministry to prepare others for ministry. Jesus began the ministry of preparation, and it continues in his name. (See "Jesus as Enabler/Preparer" for more information.)

Other than his ministry of preparation, what do we know about Jesus' teaching? First of all, we are often not given details of what he taught, only being told that he taught. We can assume that he taught about the kingdom, which he came to proclaim. We can assume that he called people to repentance (Matt 4:17).

We are definitely told about the response of the people to his teaching. First of all, they were astonished. Jesus was an ordinary person from Nazareth, not known to have received any education. How did he get such understanding? Jesus proclaimed that his teaching was not his, but was that of the One who sent him. Those who follow God will know the truth of his teaching (John 7:16-17). The people recognized that Jesus' teaching had authority that was missing from the teachings of the scribes (Matt 7:29). Sometimes people were offended by Jesus' teaching. We see an example of this when he taught at Nazareth. The people of his hometown thought they knew this young man. How dare he teach beyond their expectations (Matt 13:57)!

While many rejected Jesus because of his unexpected, nonconformist teachings, many believed (John 7:31). Jesus started with twelve disciples. As Pentecost approached, we are told that one hundred and twenty people gathered to await God's next activity (Acts 1:15). Through the earthly ministry of Jesus, which included, among other things, teaching and healing, at least one hundred and eight people were gathered into the kingdom. We might assume that others who had believed remained home at this time for fear of those who would want to eradicate the new movement of faith. But at least one hundred and twenty lives were touched and changed by Jesus' ministry. He taught as he had been prepared, and the people responded.

Jesus' teaching was not all new and unexpected. He proclaimed that he had come to fulfill the law (Matt 5:17), and his teachings demonstrated this. Jesus referred back to the leaders and Scriptures on which the practice of Judaism was based. He wanted the religious leaders to see how they had turned away from the Law of Moses and the teachings of the prophets, but it was never his intention to turn the people away from the roots of their faith.

Of course, Jesus did not just teach his inner circle. Mark 2:13 gives an account of his ministry to the masses. Jesus taught all who came to hear, and one might wonder how he made himself heard when the crowds were very large. He didn't have a sound system! Jesus taught in word and deed. Some of his "object lessons" were the feeding of the masses, his healings on the Sabbath, and his ministry to others as he hung on the cross. We see Jesus' first experience of teaching beginning when he is twelve years old, as he tries to help his parents understand the emerging priorities of his life (Luke 2:41-52), and we see his teaching continue through his life and up until death. Even after his resurrection, he gives intense preparation to his disciples as he prepares them for the new undertaking that is about to be birthed, the organism that we call the church.

When I was a Sunday school teacher, I was told to teach from the overflow of my life. Knowledge was important, but my teaching had to reflect my life and faith experience. Jesus was an example of this. His teaching, to the extent that we can witness it, did not only come from book learning. He lived what he taught, and he taught what he lived. He was committed to the One who sent him, and this was reflected in his teaching and other pastoral ministry.

Reflection Question

How important to you is the teaching ministry of the pastorate?

3

Jesus as Shepherd

Mark 10:35-40; Matthew 16:21-24;
John 13:5-10; 10:11-14, 27;
14:26; 18:10-11

> *Psalm 23:1*
> *The LORD is my shepherd, I shall not be in want.*

Shepherd is my favorite image for the pastorate, and it is the word from which we get our word, "pastor." The shepherd has many responsibilities for the flock: feeding, protecting, guiding, healing, and nurturing. A good shepherd has a relationship with the sheep, and they follow their shepherd. All of these ideas should be part of the pastorate, and Jesus certainly fulfilled each one.

Sometimes, sheep, being stubborn creatures, head in the wrong direction and have to be turned around. We see Jesus doing this with his disciples when they express wrong attitudes, such as James and John seeking to be on Jesus' right and left hands when he comes into the kingdom. Jesus—maybe not so gently—shows them two things. First, they misunderstand the kingdom of God. Second, their assertion that they are able to drink the same cup that he drinks will result in consequences with which they may not be prepared to cope. (Mark 10:35-40)

Jesus taught his disciples that following him would require denial of their lives and sacrifice, because that is what his life involved. He would lay down his life for the flock. When Peter rebukes Jesus for talking about his death (Matt 16:21-24), Shepherd Jesus has to redirect him back onto the path. Can you imagine one of the sheep rebuking the shepherd? As sheep, there are a lot of things we don't want to hear, just as there are things the flock does not like to experience (such as dips for infestations), but many things we would rather avoid are for our own good. A loving shepherd won't withhold the best simply because we don't understand its significance for us.

While it is the paradigm for servanthood, the washing of the disciples' feet (John 13:5-10) demonstrates several facets of pastoral care. A shepherd does what is necessary for bringing comfort to the sheep, and washing dusty feet with cool water would have brought comfort to Jesus' disciples. We can imagine the gentleness with which he dried their feet, maybe looking into their eyes with the overwhelming love that he demonstrated. Again, it is hard to imagine one of the sheep objecting to the shepherd's care, and yet we see Peter being a stubborn sheep.

We don't have to infer the shepherdhood of Jesus from Scriptures; Jesus proclaimed this role for himself (John 10:11-14, 27). He is not only a shepherd but also the Good Shepherd, the Shepherd who does everything right, who knows what is best for the sheep, and who is the model for every shepherd, whether of true sheep or the flock of God.

The protection offered by the Good Shepherd extends to laying down his life for the flock, which Jesus did on Calvary. There will be many faux shepherds—and indeed there were some even in Jesus' day—but none of them will willingly and intentionally give their lives for the sheep. Jesus' death is the ultimate act of protection, resulting in redemption and salvation. The Church was formed for God out of the blood of the

Good Shepherd, Jesus Christ (Acts 20:28). Is it any wonder that the leader appointed for the Church is known as "pastor," a word that comes from the idea of being a shepherd?

Jesus says that his sheep hear his voice, that he knows them, and that they follow him (John 10:27). Two-thirds of that description are appropriate for pastors today. First, the pastor is an "under-shepherd" to the Good Shepherd. The pastor must first hear and follow Jesus. Only then can the members of the local flock hear the voice of the pastor who is preaching and teaching a scripturally accurate and spiritually edifying message. When I teach, I try to emphasize that the reason for studying Scripture is to apply it to our lives; otherwise, the time spent teaching and preaching and listening is wasted. The pastor's message should always center on Christ.

Second, the pastor should know the members of the flock. With some churches, that is impossible because of size, and so "under-under-shepherds" are called to minister to smaller segments of the congregation and get to know them well. When I was an associate in a not exceptionally large church, I visited a woman who talked about her husband, whom she said was in a nursing home. She visited him every day. I reported this information to the pastor, who said that this woman, who had been part of his congregation for years, did not have a husband. I was left wondering if the woman was delusional, but then I went to visit her husband. The shepherd of the church had not taken the time to get to know at least this particular member of his flock.

The part of Jesus' description of shepherdhood that does not apply to local pastors is his remark that his sheep follow him. I don't believe that congregants should ever "follow" an earthly pastor. Jesus is still and always our Shepherd, and we should follow him alone. One of the most heartbreaking experiences I ever had was in a church that was experiencing difficulties with a fairly new pastor. The day came when that pastor stood in the front of the sanctuary and proclaimed, in effect, "All who are on my side, come up here and stand with me." That is not what the Body of Christ is supposed to be about.

When we forget who the true Shepherd is, we have stopped being part of his flock.

Even though he no longer walks the earth, the Good Shepherd continues to guide us. Jesus told his disciples, "But the Advocate, the Holy Spirit, whom the Father will send in my name, will teach you everything, and remind you of all that I have said to you" (John 14:26). These words are just as true for us today.

When sheep stray from the path, shepherds lay their staffs on the sheep's sides and gently guide them onto the right way. It is truly an art for the pastor to learn how to redirect the members of God's flock without harsh criticism and negativity. I haven't learned the art of that yet, so for now I mostly try to avoid redirecting people unless absolutely necessary. If this needs to happen, I recommend utlizing other servant ministers in the congregation, such as the deacons, to talk with the wayward individuals and guide them in a loving way.

Finally, the shepherd protects the sheep. The shepherd must be ever alert for predators. The enemy will sneak into the fold and try to lead the sheep astray or destroy the sheep. When Peter draws a sword to defend Jesus from those who have come to arrest him, Jesus stops him, but not before Peter strikes home with a swipe to Malchus's ear (John 18:10-11). Had Jesus not healed the ear and called for forbearance, the situation might have been much worse.

In his greatest act of spiritual protection, Jesus won victory on Calvary over the powers of darkness that would strive to destroy the church and the Body of Christ. It is now up to the flock to walk in his protection by submitting to God and resisting the enemy (Jas 4:7). The Good Shepherd continues to protect, guide, and care for the flock of God.

Reflection Question

Are you familiar with all the shepherd elements of the pastorate?

4

Jesus as Evangelist

Matthew 4:17, 23; 6:33; 10:7;
Mark 10:14; Parables

> *2 Timothy 4:5*
> *But you, keep your head in all situations, endure hardship,*
> *do the work of an evangelist, discharge all the duties of your ministry.*

"The church today is raising a whole generation of mules. They know how to sweat and to work hard, but they don't know how to reproduce themselves."[1]

Evangelism is the process of sharing the message of God's kingdom so that others may enter. This was the main mission of Jesus' life on earth. While he lived, he continuously pointed others to the kingdom of God. Through his death, he opened the door for all to come in. Jesus reproduced his life within the lives of those who shared his earthly ministry, and he continues to invite others into the kingdom through the witness of faithful followers.

John the Baptizer was appointed from before his conception to prepare the way for Jesus. John preached a baptism of repentance unto the forgiveness of sin (Matt 3). When

John's life ended, Jesus assumed this ministry of proclamation, calling people to repentance, for the kingdom of heaven had come near (Matt 4:17, 23). Jesus not only proclaimed the kingdom but also demonstrated the kingdom. Everything about his life pointed people to this grand ideal of a people who live in God's ways, caring for each other, loving God and others, and doing everything in the name of Christ.

In a section of his Sermon on the Mount, Jesus talks about the things people worry about: clothing, food, and shelter. He gives examples of God's faithful provision through nature, questioning why people should worry about such things. But he culminates this list by admonishing people to seek first the kingdom of God. Why? Because if God's kingdom is truly our focus and our heart's desire, all the other things we think we need will be given to us (Matt 6:25-33), along with a few desires here and there.

Jesus, always the teacher, encouraged his disciples to be evangelists. In Matthew 10:7, he tells them, "As you go, proclaim the good news, 'The kingdom of heaven has come near.'" While his disciples proclaimed the gospel in words, Jesus' evangelism took place through words and actions.

When Jesus healed, he demonstrated that the kingdom of heaven is life and health. When Jesus fed people, he demonstrated that the kingdom is sufficient for every need. And as he died on the cross, he demonstrated that the kingdom welcomes all who will come, even those whose lives have not previously honored God; that the kingdom offers forgiveness; and that the kingdom cares about the humblest people, even widows without resources.

One of the favorite stories of Sunday school teachers shows that even children were welcomed into the kingdom. As parents brought their children to be blessed by Jesus, Jesus welcomed them with open arms (Mark 10:14).

Many pastors today do not actively engage in evangelism. When we minister to congregations consisting mostly of people who have been in church all their lives, it seems unnecessary to invite people into God's kingdom. From personal experience, however, I know that not everyone who fills the pews on Sunday morning is a member of the kingdom. I sat in church for years before coming to Christ and entering the kingdom of God. For this reason, I try to sprinkle my preaching repertoire with occasional evangelistic messages.

Jesus lived a life of evangelism—his life and death were geared toward bringing people into God's kingdom. I have always preferred a certain type of evangelism, and I think Jesus practiced it: lifestyle evangelism. This is a means of spreading the gospel message by the way we live. Jesus did this beautifully, but he also had another unique way of sharing the gospel message through parables.

One of the frustrations of my preaching ministry is finding appropriate stories with which to introduce or highlight my messages. If I could create parables like Jesus did, I would have no problem. Jesus used messages that were framed within the understanding and lifestyles of the people to whom he spoke, although they were not always easy to understand.

Often Jesus' parables began with a simile: "The kingdom of heaven is like . . . ." At various times, he compared it to a mustard seed, yeast, a merchant in search of fine pearls, a net thrown into the sea, the master of a household, and a landowner. All of these things, found mostly in Matthew 33, were familiar to the common people who listened to Jesus. The difficulty came in his application of these common items to kingdom life. For example, how does the leavening that occurs when a woman mixes yeast with three measures of flour relate to the kingdom of heaven? Jesus' listeners probably understood the intent of these parables more than we do today.

One of my favorite kingdom parables is the parable of the sower (Matt 13:4-9). What does the seed represent? What do the bird that eats the seed, the rocky ground, the thorns, and the fruit represent? Fortunately—and this may be why it is one of my favorites—Jesus explains his comparisons in the following verses. The seed is the word of the kingdom, or the word of God. The bird is the evil one who snatches the seed away before it has a chance to sprout. The rocky ground is the heart that receives the message with joy, but there is no root. Troubles come, like the sun withering a vine, and the seed withers and dies. The thorns are the cares of the world that choke out the message. The seed does not die—these people do not turn away—but there is no fruit produced. Even though Jesus explains this parable (Matt 13:19-23), some of us are still left with questions. For instance, does the dying of the seed mean the loss of salvation? Sometimes we must be content with our questions and trust that Jesus will continue to clarify his intent.

The most evangelistic "lesson" of Jesus' life was his death. Through his death and resurrection, Jesus opened the way for all to receive life. His life, his witness, his death, and his resurrection point to the kingdom of God. It is open to all who will receive and enter.

Reflection Question

How important is bringing people into God's Kingdom in your church?

Note

[1]"Evangelism," in *1001 Humorous Illustrations,* ed. Michael Hodgins (Grand Rapids: Zondervan, 1992), 136.

5
Jesus as Enabler/Preparer

*John 21:15-25; 14:12; 20:21-22;
Luke 10:1-11; 24:49*

> *2 Timothy 4:2*
> *Preach the Word; be prepared in season and out of season;*
> *correct, rebuke and encourage—with great patience and careful instruction.*

One of the most difficult and yet possibly most rewarding aspects of the calling of a pastor is to enable people to minister to others and prepare them for that ministry. I have seen bulletins that say that all people are ministers, but few truly have a clue as to what that means. Sometimes, the statement is simply not true.

Jesus enabled and prepared others for ministry. His ministry on earth was as much a "ministry of preparation" as it was anything else. He took a group of twelve diverse, mostly uneducated men and enabled them to be leaders of the church that was to be.

In the beautiful story of Peter's restoration, John 21:15-25, we see the paradigm of enabling. Peter was devastated because he had denied Jesus. Three times he denied knowing the man whom he loved and had followed for about three years. He had sworn that he would never do it, and yet, when faced with a potential threat to his life, he readily and vehemently denied that he knew the One who was about to give his life for him. Matthew 26:75 tells us that, reminded of Jesus' prediction that he would do exactly what he had done, Peter wept bitterly.

When word came of the empty tomb and evidence was given of the resurrection, Peter must have felt that, if Jesus was indeed alive, he would want nothing to do with Peter because of his denial. We are told that there was a meeting between Jesus and Simon (Luke 24:34; "Simon" is part of Peter's name), but we are given no details of that meeting. It must have been emotional and reconciliatory, because in John 21, Peter is anxious to see Jesus once he recognizes the Resurrected Lord on the beach.

Peter had denied Jesus three times, so Jesus gives Peter three opportunities to affirm his commitment to ministry for Jesus. Each time Jesus calls Peter to feed his lambs or sheep, Jesus is calling him to forget his failures and look forward to what God has prepared for him. While Pentecost was the final stage of Peter's preparation, through this little fellowship on the beach, Jesus begins enabling Peter to lead the church that will arise.

In Luke 10:1-11, we see something that is given little explanation, and yet it speaks volumes about Jesus' ministry as enabler. Usually we see Jesus focused on twelve men. In the Luke 10 passage, we see that Jesus sends out seventy people, two by two. These people are to go to the cities Jesus will be visiting. They are, in fact, the successors of John the Baptizer, preparing the way for Jesus' visits.

I used to participate in the visitation ministry of a church I attended. Almost every Tuesday afternoon, I experienced abdominal pain in anticipation of this evening ministry, but once I got started on visits, I was fine. Sometimes it was little more than a social call, but occasionally we would get to share the gospel with someone who had visited our church. It was rewarding, and it prepared me for something I could not imagine at the time: visits I would make as a pastor.

Who were these 70 men and women? Were they new believers or people who had been long steeped in Jewish law? We are told that, at the festival of Pentecost following Jesus' ascension, 120 people waited for God's call (Acts 1:15). Were these 70 part of that 120, or had some fallen away and others joined? The composition of this group is unknown to us, but the way Jesus prepared them for ministry is clear.

First, Jesus gave them their purpose: to find laborers for the harvest of the kingdom. They were to try to bring people into the kingdom of God. Jesus told them that they would be susceptible to dangers, referring to them as lambs amid wolves. They were to go to one house in the city they visited and stay there, unless they were not welcomed. They were not to question the food they were offered—it could have been leftovers from food presented to idols, but that was not their concern. They were to speak peace to the homes they visited, and the peace that was there would return to them. They were to proclaim the kingdom and to demonstrate the presence of the kingdom by curing the sick. These seventy people were enabled to go forth in the full power of God, and apparently they were successful. We are told in Luke 10:17 that the seventy returned with joy, remarking even on the submission of demons to the name of Jesus. Jesus gave them authority to walk in kingdom life, and they walked in that authority and saw victory.

As Jesus prepared to leave the earth following his resurrection, he gave some parting words to his disciples (Luke 24:49). He told them that he would send what the Father had promised. If they waited, they would receive power from on high that would come upon them as clothing. The coming of the Holy Spirit is the fulfillment of this promise. The twelve disciples had received a small taste of enablement prior to Jesus' ascension (John 20:21-22). Jesus told them that they were being sent as he had been sent, and then he breathed the Spirit upon them. This was not an indwelling, as they received at Pentecost, but it was an external empowerment to get them through the interim time. Jesus knew that his followers would have to deal with fear, maybe persecution, and possibly ridicule, so he enabled them to stand against whatever the world would bring their way. Once they received the Holy Spirit (Acts 2:4), they had everything they needed to continue their ministry, completing the preparation that Jesus began when he called them from their boats and tax-collecting booths.

Jesus' ministry of enablement and preparation continues today. When his disciples are struggling to understand, he assures them, "Very truly, I tell you, the one who believes in me will also do the works that I do and, in fact, will do greater works than these, because I am going to the Father" (John 14:12). Believing in Jesus is the beginning of the preparation period that lasts as long as we walk this earth. How has Jesus enabled us? By leaving his Holy Spirit. That is the significance of his departure to be with the Father. Jesus had to leave so that the Spirit could come, and it is by the enablement of the Spirit that we can do greater works than Jesus did. Jesus' preparation and enablement is given to all who believe, not just to pastors and church leaders. By the power of the Holy Spirit, Jesus enables us to go forth into our corners of the world and bear witness to all that has been given to us.

Reflection Question

Are people in your congregation being identified and prepared for ministry which might be awaiting them?

6

Jesus as Caregiver

Mark 1:30-31; John 19:26-27

> *John 21:16*
> *Again Jesus said, "Simon son of John, do you truly love me?"*
> *He answered, "Yes, Lord, you know that I love you."*
> *Jesus said, "Take care of my sheep."*

Even though I have always been quite uncomfortable in personal, social conversations, I find myself relishing most times when I can visit members of my congregation, whether in their homes or, more likely, in hospitals and nursing homes. At the beginning of my first called pastorate, I discovered myself in the midst of a death ministry. I saw the Lord giving me many abilities I was previously unaware of, abilities with which to care for people in sickness and sorrow.

Numerous Scriptures teach of Jesus' ministry to masses, but his ministry of caring to individuals is informative for us. In Mark 1:30-31, we see the story of Jesus' ministry to Peter's mother-in-law. He had just ministered to the crowds, but then he was made aware of the illness of a disciple's relative.

Several points in this brief passage can guide those of us who do sickbed ministry.

First of all, Jesus doesn't do a lot of talking. He takes the woman by the hand and lifts her from her bed. As he does so, her fever breaks and she is made well. Often, people who visit the sick seem to feel that somehow their conversation and presence will make the sick ones whole. They act as if the more they talk, the more likely the person is to get well. What our sick and sorrowing friends need is not our conversation but the touch of Jesus. We should certainly offer words of prayer through which the touch may come. Beyond that, conversation may actually be a detriment to the well-being of the patients.

Second, Jesus doesn't pity this woman. As she heads toward the kitchen, Jesus doesn't say, "Now you take it easy. We don't want you overdoing it." Instead, Jesus allows her to serve him and the others present. In recovery from sickness, and especially sorrow, the best thing we might encourage people to do is engage in some activity. As committee members consider helpers for a project, I have heard things like, "We don't want to ask them to help because of what they are going through." We should give people the privilege of letting them choose for themselves what they can do in a time of difficulty. Neglecting them because of their current situation may cause more harm. Pity is debilitating and encourages self-pity and other negative attitudes. We have to act within reason, of course, but we should never try to discourage people from doing things that they think they are able to do. And we should always be available with a helping hand in case they struggle.

Caregiving may take many unexpected forms. In John 19:26-27, Jesus demonstrates caring for his mother from the cross. His actions can't heal her sorrowful heart or restore him as her son, but they can provide for her future needs. A widow in Jesus' day faced humiliation and desperation and could often be forced into compromising situations if she had no children to care for her. Jesus takes care of that need for his mother.

We know that Jesus had other brothers and sisters (Mark 3:32). Why, then, did he entrust his mother into the hands of one of his disciples rather than one of his siblings? I tend to believe that Jesus was thinking not so much in familial terms as in faith terms. John was perhaps the disciple who was closest to Jesus, and he may have had the kind of faith that Jesus would want modeled for a loved one. In other words, Jesus gave his mother into the hands of one who loved him and whom he knew would love his mother. Through John, Mary would also have access to the faith community that Jesus knew would soon spring up.

     We should find deep meaning in the fact that, as Jesus went through his most difficult hour, he thought of other people. We see in several places that, although Jesus was weary, he never failed to care for those who came to him with needs. Very often in ministry, we let weariness or, worse, days off keep us from ministering to others. We have to care for ourselves, and Jesus did this, but we must always be open to the ways we can meet the needs of others, despite our weariness and personal needs.

Reflection Question

Is pastoral care of shut-ins, elderly, sick, and marginalized a prominent part of ministry in your church?

7

Jesus as Sacrificer and Sacrifice

John 10:15; 2 Corinthians 5:21;
1 Peter 2:24; Hebrews 2:17

> *Philippians 2:17*
> *But even if I am being poured out like a drink offering*
> *on the sacrifice and service coming from your faith, I am glad*
> *and rejoice with all of you.*

We don't often hear the word "sacrifice," especially in ministry. Sometimes I get the impression that pastors and church leaders think that their congregations exist to serve them. But *we* are to be the ones who serve, who must sometimes make great sacrifices for the good of our congregations. Jesus continually demonstrated this.

Jesus is the Good Shepherd. He does everything necessary for the good of the sheep, including laying down his life for them (John 10:15). In the face of predators, a shepherd must be willing to give his all for the benefit of the flock. The church today has many predators, and one of the roles of the undershepherd is to be on guard against threats and either lead the congregation away from the threat or enable them to stand against it.

Second Corinthians 5:21 is a Scripture I love, although I don't understand it. I know that Jesus bore our sin on the cross, so that helps me understand how he could become sin. He was willing to bear the burden of our sin, to become our sin, so that we would not have to pay the cost for our sin. That is a sacrifice beyond comprehension. What I don't understand about this passage is how we become the righteousness of God. As pastors, the best we can do is bear the burdens of our congregants (Gal 6:2), but we don't become as they are when we bear their burdens. Only Jesus can demonstrate the unconditional sacrifice of becoming sin for us.

First Peter 2:24 is a little easier to understand in light of righteousness. Because of Jesus' sacrifice, we can live for righteousness. It gets difficult, from time to time, to remember that it is not our own righteousness. As pastors and believers, we should always walk in the righteousness of Christ. Right thinking, right speaking, right attitudes, and right actions should be the goal of all who are in Christ.

We often forget that because of the sacrifice of Christ, we have healing. We have to choose to walk in this healing, but it is always available to us. We are healed by the stripes of Christ (e.g., 1 Pet 2:24). Sickness and disease are not from God; they are tools of Satan. By the name and authority of Jesus Christ, we can stand against these results of sin and walk in the health and wholeness that God desires for us. We can encourage others to walk in the healing of Christ by our example and faithful teaching, and Jesus Christ, our Sacrifice, enables us to do this.

We can best appreciate the sacrificial work of Jesus when we understand that he became one of us in order to understand what we as humans are made of. A pastor has to be able to understand his or her congregants. I try to take part in as many activities as possible, like bringing food for fellowships or attending events, just to get to know the people I serve. I try not to hold myself above anything or anyone. I even attend the events I don't enjoy—like meetings—so I can know what is going on in the congregation. Hebrews 2:17 tells us that our faithful high priest, Jesus the Christ, went to the extreme in order to be an effective and meaningful sacrifice for us. My efforts are a small way to honor what Christ did.

Reflection Question

Sacrifice is not a popular concept today. Is the pastorate of your church a sacrificial pastorate?

8

Jesus as Social Activist

Luke 7:11-16; Matthew 14:15-21

> *Amos 5:24*
> *But let justice roll on like a river, righteousness like a never-failing stream!*

I have to confess that, as I understand the concept, "social ministry" is not a strong point for me. I view it as the mission to help all people have the rights that they deserve as human beings, such as food, shelter, and safety. I think all pastors find a point of focus for their ministry, and mine has been helping those who claim to know Christ understand what that truly means and how it should be represented in our lives. While there is certainly a social aspect to my focus, "social ministry" as it is often defined today can't be the whole focus of the church, and it was not the whole focus of Jesus' ministry.

Jesus did, however, express and demonstrate views of how we are to treat the people in our community who are not always able to care for themselves.

Deuteronomy 26:12-13 is one of many Old Testament passages that talks about how the Israelites were to care for the less fortunate among them. Widows represent one such group. As we saw earlier, a widow without children to care for her could find herself in desperate circumstances. The New Testament offers two examples of Jesus' ministry to widows. The first was the way he cared for his own mother as he was dying on the cross (see "Jesus as Caregiver"). In Luke 7:11-16, we see the other example. As Jesus is journeying, he encounters a funeral entourage. Immediately understanding the situation, he has compassion for the mother of the deceased. She is a widow, and the dead person was her only child, so she is now in dire circumstances. Jesus, master of compassion, has compassion—not pity—for this woman, and he restores life to her son. She no longer has to depend on the mercy of others. Her son is able to care for her, as expected of children at that time.

As believers, we are unlikely to restore life to the deceased children of our friends, and this is no longer necessary as it was in Jesus' time; our society provides means whereby people can be cared for when their families are unable to care for them. One of our social responsibilities as the church might be to make sure that these resources are fulfilling needs in a way that respects the dignity and the rights of those who are served.

Another social ministry of the church might be supporting local food pantries and soup kitchens. We see two examples in Scripture of Jesus setting up ad-hoc food pantries: the feedings of the 5,000 (Matt 14:15-21) and the 4,000 (Matt 15:32-38). Jesus and his disciples did not collect and bring food in anticipation of meeting needs. The food was produced by the disciples at the time of need, and one account says that a child offered his lunch (John 6:9) to the disciples. The actual food produced amounted to a few fish and some bread, hardly enough to feed such large groups of people—at least by natural standards. As the food was passed around, however, it miraculously multiplied, and all the people were fed.

The spiritual symbolism in the stories of the feedings

is that Jesus, the Bread of Life, gave himself for others and that his life was sufficient for all. But there is also, of course, a social message. When we are aware of needs, we must do what we can to meet those needs.

I believe that Jesus also taught powerful lessons through these miraculous feedings. In each account, the disciples complain of the paucity of food for so many people. They have seen Jesus do miracles through them, but at this moment they seem to have forgotten what they saw. Jesus tells them to feed the people. As they begin to comply with Jesus' command, they see the people being fed. They surely are aware of the food multiplying as they give it out. Once again, Jesus demonstrates his ability—and his willingness—to meet needs. It takes his disciples a while, however, to learn that they don't have to worry about needs. We can learn faith from the disciples' lack of faith.

Reflection Question

Is your congregation meeting the needs of the oppressed, neglected, and abandoned?

9

Jesus as Tradition Breaker

Matthew 15:1-20; 5:17

> *2 Corinthians 6:17*
> *"Therefore come out from them and be separate, says the Lord...."*

As a bit of a rebel myself, I can appreciate the tradition-breaking aspect of Jesus' life. I think pastors have to be a bit rebellious. If we always go along with the status quo, if we are only willing to do or be what others expect us to do or be, it is likely that we are not faithfully following Jesus. The world has gotten such a foothold in our churches that expectations are frequently world based rather than faith based.

In Matthew 15:1-20, we see an example of Jesus trying to get the religious leaders to understand what he is all about. He has to help them see where they are so that they might see where they can be.

First of all, the scribes and Pharisees have noticed that Jesus' disciples do not go through the ritual washing before they eat. The custom was to wash hands and feet, and certain water was always provided for this ritual. So they confront Jesus about the breach of their religious etiquette.

Jesus doesn't apologize for his disciples. Instead, he turns the tables on the religious leaders. He asks them why they break God's commandments for the sake of their traditions. Then he cites an example of how they break the commandment to honor father and mother. He calls the Pharisees and scribes hypocrites, quoting Isaiah, who taught that the people made the rules of humanity more important than God's rules. Then Jesus returns to the idea of hand washing. People are not defiled by what goes into their mouths, he says, but by what is already in their hearts.

When Jesus uses the word "defile," he is speaking in religious terms. He is not addressing the health issues that were even more rampant and dangerous in his day than they are in ours. He was referring instead to the belief that religious impurity was caused by not following rules. Jesus knew, as we do today, that illness and disease can come from what goes into our mouths. No loving pastor would tell people that they should give no thought to what goes into their bodies or the condition of the hands that bring food to the body. Jesus is speaking of religion, not health issues.

Jesus wants the religious leaders and his disciples to understand that we are defiled not by what goes into our bodies through our mouths but by the words, attitudes, and actions that come from unclean hearts. The Pharisees put their faith in visible obedience to the law, not in attitudes. Jesus was trying to get them to see a different way, but their traditions bound them too tightly.

The religious leaders of Jesus' day held to rituals and behaviors that had a basis in the Law of Moses and in the teachings of the prophets. These teachings came from God, and so, as a foundation for their religion, they had great value. But teachers throughout the centuries since Moses and Isaiah had so expanded and stretched the foundation that the laws lost their original intent. People like the scribes and Pharisees followed rules without understanding their significance and basis. They obeyed the words without remembering or understanding the intent. Jesus came to help them understand.

In Matthew 5:17, Jesus asserts that he did not come to abolish the laws or prophets but to fulfill them. The religious leaders certainly did not see Jesus' ministry in this way. They viewed him as a threat to everything they held dear. Any pastor who comes teaching the way of God rather than the ways of people will put herself under threat of misunderstanding. The caution, of course, is that we need to make sure, as Jesus did, that we are teaching God's ways rather than our own, that we are following the true teachings of Scripture instead of our own interpretations. Most of the religious leaders never saw beyond Jesus' upsetting of their religious strongholds. They never understood how his rebellion could lead them in the way of righteousness. If Jesus remained misunderstood by those who heard him, we can expect that we will also be misunderstood.

But we are not called to be understood. We are called to be faithful.

Reflection Question

Are you conformed to this world or have you been transformed?

10

Jesus as Embracer

Matthew 19:13-14; 9:9-12;
Luke 19:2-9

> *Mark 9:37*
> *"Whoever welcomes one of these little children in my name welcomes me; and whoever welcomes me does not welcome me but the one who sent me."*

Who doesn't like a warm, welcoming hug, especially in the face of rejection and humiliation by others? Several stories about Jesus in Scriptures demonstrate his ability to embrace others, whether in a physical sense or in a more spiritual or emotional sense.

Most children who have heard the story of Jesus in Matthew 19:13-14 responded positively to it. We see the same idea in Mark 10:13 and Luke 18:15. Jesus welcomes children into his presence and is willing to draw them close, even to touch them. I picture Jesus opening his arms wide to welcome and bless these little ones.

Children in Jesus' day were not the precious, beloved blessing to families that they are often considered today.

Children were valued for working in the fields and for increasing the esteem of the father who had many, but they were essentially nonentities in society. That is why the disciples were against letting the children approach Jesus. Why would an important teacher like Jesus want to spend time with children? Jesus, contradicting the beliefs of the disciples, said that children were the substance of the kingdom of God. Indeed, in other Scriptures, we are told that unless we become like children, we will have no part of the kingdom (e.g., Matt 18:2-5). I think the children who were brought into Jesus' arms went away knowing how precious and beloved they were.

But Jesus didn't only embrace children. Luke 19:2-9 tells the wonderful story of Zacchaeus. He was a vertically impaired tax collector who was also wealthy—probably due to his tax collecting. Because he abused his profession, he certainly faced the rejection of his people. One day, Zacchaeus heard that Jesus was coming to town, and he wanted to see him. It probably never occurred to him that Jesus would want to see Zacchaeus, but he did. Calling him down from the tree that Zacchaeus had climbed for a better vantage point, Jesus invited himself to Zacchaeus's home. Zacchaeus welcomed Jesus gladly, but the welcome he received from Jesus changed his life. Because Jesus stopped to spend time with this rejected citizen, Zacchaeus received an emotional hug that brought repentance and salvation to his life. We don't hear anything more of Zacchaeus, but, because of Jesus' words of salvation, we know that his life was changed.

Zacchaeus did not become one of the twelve disciples who ministered with and followed Jesus for three years, but there is another story of Jesus welcoming a tax collector who did become one of those twelve. In Matthew 9:9-12, Matthew is in his tax-collecting booth when Jesus approaches him. We are told nothing of Matthew's tax-collecting practices. Scriptures such as Matthew 11:19 indicate that tax collectors were not highly esteemed: "the Son of Man came eating and drinking, and they say, 'Look, a glutton and a drunkard, a friend of tax collectors and sinners!' Yet wisdom is vindicated by her deeds." In this verse, the people distinguish "tax collectors" from all other sinners, showing the disdain they feel for those who do that type of work. Matthew probably had few friends, and we only hear of him in the lists of all the other disciples. But Jesus looked past the attitudes of the citizens and called Matthew to be one of his disciples, welcoming him into an exclusive, unique fellowship. I am sure Matthew felt the welcoming touch of Jesus on his heart. He immediately left his tax booth and followed Jesus. And we now have the Gospel that bears his name, revealing Jesus as King.

Every pastor needs to have a welcoming, embracing heart. Sometimes that may take him or her beyond the attitudes and wishes of the group that he or she is serving. One example is John Woolman, a Quaker who was an early abolitionist. An itinerant preacher, he encountered opposition to his anti-slavery views everywhere he went. When he accepted the hospitality of slave holders, he insisted on paying the slaves for their services to him. Gradually, and through the Friends' tradition of seeking the leading of the Spirit, Woolman was able to convince the Quakers that slavery was not pleasing to the Lord God.[1] His open, embracing attitude allowed him to see the humanity of those whom society had oppressed, and he was able to inspire a great change in the views of his fellow believers.

Reflection Question

Is hugging or embracing a common part of the life of your congregation?

Note

[1] *Wikipedia*, s.v. "The Journal of John Woolman" (1774), en.wikipedia.org/wiki/John_Woolman (accessed July 2013).

11

Jesus as Intercessor

John 17

> *Hebrews 7:25*
> *Therefore he is able to save completely those who come to God through him, because he always lives to intercede for them.*

At least once weekly, I go into the sanctuary of our church building, and I pray for the congregation that I am called to serve. I stand in intercession for these people, praying for their protection, asking God that they will experience and show Christ-like love, and bringing up any other needs that I have sensed. The people aren't there when I pray for them, but I have no doubt that, through the Spirit, my prayers will reach out into their lives as I pray. I also believe that, again through the Spirit, my prayers may linger and pour down upon them as they are present in the building.

Every pastor should intercede for the people he or she serves. John 17 offers an extensive example of Jesus' prayer of intercession for himself, for the disciples who currently served with him, and for those who would come to believe through their ministry. I consider this chapter to be the true "Lord's Prayer," compared to the one commonly known as the Lord's Prayer, which is actually more of a "Disciples' Prayer" (Matt 6:9ff; Luke 11:1ff). And I believe that Jesus' prayer extends down to us today.

Christ's prayer of intercession begins with prayer for himself, which, though it's not technically intercession, needs to be addressed. I have heard people say that they don't think they should pray for themselves. In the Wednesday night prayer time at our church, we hand out bookmarks that bear the names of everyone in our congregation. Sometimes people get the section in which their own names are listed. The fact that they skip over their names, or the way they pray for themselves, shows that this is an uncomfortable experience for them. But we have several examples of Jesus praying for himself; two of these instances are in the upper room in John 17 and in Gethsemane in Matthew 26:36-45. It seems strange that we don't follow his model. If Jesus needed to pray for himself and his ministry and mission on earth, how much more should we pray for ourselves?

As pastors, it seems natural to seek God's help as we strive to follow God, to lead the people we serve, and to make sure that our lives are examples. Jesus couldn't do his ministry on his own. How dare we think that we can?

Following his prayer for himself, Jesus begins interceding for his disciples (v. 6). Intercession is standing in the gap for someone and representing that person to others. A lawyer intercedes for his clients, and a family advocate may intercede for an abused child. Jesus is standing before the throne of God, representing his disciples and, later, all believers. When we put such intercession into the form of prayer, it becomes intercessory prayer.

Jesus reminds his Father that these people are a gift to Jesus from God. Both God and Christ share responsibility for those who have kept the Father's word. Jesus says that he is not praying for the world; he is praying for those who have been given to him. He prays that the Father will prepare them for his upcoming absence. He prays for their protection by the Name of the Father. Jesus says that he has been protecting them while he was with them—and even, apparently, when he sent them out apart from himself. Jesus prays that those he has loved and cared for may have the full measure of his joy within them. What a great thing to pray for the people with whom we work: not only for their safety and preparation but also for their *joy*.

Then, knowing that the world will hate his followers as he was hated, Jesus seeks their protection from the Ruler of the world, the evil one. He doesn't ask that they be taken from the world; he prays that they are protected while they are in it. In verse 17, Jesus asks that his current disciples be sanctified by the truth, God's word. On Pentecost, this particular request is fulfilled (see Acts 2). As 120 disciples went forth by the power of the Spirit, proclaiming the word of God, they were strengthened in their faith and thus their ability to stand against the evil one.

In John 17:20, Jesus tells the Father that his prayer is not only for his current disciples but for all those who "will believe" in him through their message. That applied to the people to whom the disciples directly ministered, and it applies to us as we read the Gospels, the letters by Paul and Peter, and the account of the newly developing church in Acts. On that night before his crucifixion, Jesus was praying for us.

As Jesus prays for all the disciples to come, he asks for unity, which is probably the last thing many are seeking (vv. 21-23). As long as we allow the Body of Christ to be divided by denominations, diversity of color, social standing, economic status, and theological viewpoints—to name just a few of our many divisions—we prevent the answer to that prayer. Only when we put our differences aside and seek the unity that comes in Christ can we see the fulfillment of Jesus' petition on our behalf. Jesus says that he has given us the ability to be united, but we have denied that ability.

Then Jesus prays that we might be with him (v. 24). What a wonderful hope! To see his glory and to abide in his visible presence should be the longing of our hearts, and we look forward to its fulfillment. Jesus says, however, that we might be with him "where he is." I like that. As he prayed, he was still in the world, and his Spirit lingers here. Even as we walk this earth, we can be with Jesus because Jesus is here. We don't have to wait until we get to heaven to be with Jesus. We should be walking with Jesus every hour of every day of our lives.

The closing of this prayer for believers is beautiful (vv. 25-26). Jesus has made the Father known to us. I believe that, in this process, Jesus has also made us known to the Father. We are not some ephemeral idea floating around in Jesus' head. Jesus speaks about those who will believe through the disciples as if we were with him just as the disciples were. We are real and viable to Jesus as he prays for us. If we ever feel that we are not precious or beloved in God's sight, this prayer should change our minds.

Romans 8:26 and 34 tell us that Jesus continues to intercede for us. As we pray for ourselves and others, we don't always know how to pray. Jesus has experienced our weaknesses and knows exactly what we are going through. As we face our own difficulties, as we lift our hearts in intercession for others, Jesus is already interceding for us before the Father. What a wonderful demonstration of pastoral care. What a wonderful example for pastors who have a heart for the needs and concerns of their parishioners! Thank you, Jesus.

Reflection Question

Is intercessory prayer an ongoing part of your congregational life?

12

Jesus as Servant

John 13

> *Galatians 5:13*
> *You, my brothers, were called to be free. But do not use your freedom to indulge the sinful nature; rather, serve one another in love.*

I like to think of myself as a servant who tries to do things for the people I serve beyond the "required" ministry. I desire to do things that people may not actually be aware of—and don't even need to know about—but that affect their lives in some way. As much as I seek servanthood, however, I don't think I could make a practice of washing people's feet. Of course, in our culture, it is not as much of a necessity as it was in Jesus' day. We might wear sandals, but generally, we have paved roads, and walking is not our normal mode of transportation. We don't walk through the muck and mire of everyday living, as the people of Jesus' day did. And even if our feet get dirty, we can simply step into the shower or tub and quickly get clean.

There can be no greater example of servanthood than the one found in John 13. Jesus and his followers had gathered for an evening meal, just prior to the Passover. Verse 3 sets the stage beautifully: "Jesus, knowing that the Father had given all things into his hands, and that he had come from God and was going to God . . . ." What greater remark could be made about someone? What more exalted concept could we have of another than that, having come from God, such a person had everything placed in his or her hands? Yet what does this honored person do? Does he flaunt his status over his followers? Does he insist on being served? No, he takes upon himself the task of the most humble servant, the washing of his companions' feet.

What a beautiful example for pastors: not to think of themselves more highly than they ought, but to consider others as better than themselves. Let's look at the details of this service to Jesus' companions in ministry.

When all are assembled, Jesus gets up, takes off his outer clothing, and dons a towel. The undergarments are short, and so Jesus puts himself in a compromising position as he begins serving his followers. The men—we don't think there were any women present at that time—are reclining on couches around a central table, so Jesus has to stoop down to wash their feet. This makes him even more vulnerable, considering his lack of clothing and the fact that he dried their feet with the towel wrapped around his waist. But it doesn't seem to bother him.

Consider who was there: not only the beloved disciples but also the one Jesus knew would betray him. What powerful love this shows—a pastor washing the feet of his greatest earthly enemy. But it is not Judas who tries to stop Jesus in his mission; it is Peter. In verse 6, Peter asks, "Are you going to wash my feet?" The implication is that there is no way he will allow Jesus to wash his feet. Jesus tells Peter that he may not understand now, but he will later. Peter's rejection of Jesus' gift then becomes more adamant: "You shall never wash my feet!" Poor Peter! He hasn't learned that his way is not yet God's way, and that sometimes silence is better than outbursts.

I wonder how Jesus spoke the words of verse 8. When he said, "Unless I wash you, you have no part with me," did he speak in sorrow, in pain, or in anger? Did he look Peter straight in the eye, or did he drop his eyes to the ground? Sometimes pastors have to point out truths to congregants, and we know that they may not respond well. How we speak to them makes all the difference.

Regardless of the tone or body language, Jesus speaks these words in love, and Peter responds, like Peter usually does, in an abundance of exuberation. He asks Jesus to wash not only his feet but his hands and head as well.

But Jesus says that washing the feet is enough.

Having finished washing everyone's feet, Jesus dresses and returns to the table. Then he brings the object lesson into focus as he asks them if they understand what he has done for them (v. 12). "Sure, you washed our feet," they might have acknowledged, although we aren't told what they said or if they responded at all. Jesus proceeds to explain that he did more than clean dirty feet. He gave his disciples an example of how they are to treat one another. They should wash each other's feet not only to learn to care for one another but also in order to become servants. If they become servants to each other, they will better be able to serve those who will come into the church that is soon to be formed. The greatest among them became their servant, and blessing will come to those who never consider themselves the greatest among the group but are always willing to be servants to others.

Reflection Question

Is service freely given among the members of your congregation?

13

Jesus as Organizer

Matthew 10:1-16;
Luke 6:13; John 15:16

> *1 Peter 4:10*
> *Each one should use whatever gift he has received to serve others, faithfully administering God's grace in its various forms.*

I recently asked people to describe some of the gifts they felt they had. Few of the ones I asked were able to move beyond "administration." Some people within the congregation are great at details, some make good proofreaders, and some are adept organizers. A pastor should have some organizational skills and be organized and methodical, but I don't think that administration is a gift many have.

In Matthew 10:1-16, Luke 6:13, and John 15:16, we will look at some of Jesus' organizational skills. Jesus was not "too heavenly minded to be any earthly good." He considered practical ways to do ministry, and then he went about his plan.

In the Matthew passage, Jesus prepares his disciples for a mission: to go out with the authority he gives them and to drive out evil spirits and heal every disease and sickness. This is similar to the passage in Luke 10, which we looked at in "Jesus as Enabler/Preparer," but now we will study different aspects of this sending out. In the earlier case, Jesus sent out seventy people, a larger group. In Matthew, Jesus is sending his closest disciples, those whom he is specifically preparing to be the leaders of the new church.

Jesus is delegating authority. He doesn't feel that he has to do everything by himself. He knows that the time will come when he won't be there, and so he is preparing these twelve to follow in his footsteps. He is taking a group of people who are essentially volunteers and preparing them to be leaders. How he goes about this demonstrates his organizational skills.

First, Jesus gives them their mission: in this case, it is to stand against evil and to heal. Then there is a list of the disciples who are sent out. Record keeping is important for any organization. Next, Jesus gives them detailed instructions. They are told where to go and where not to go. He tells them the specific message they are to preach. He also instructs them to take nothing with them; provisions should come from their ministry. He explains what they should expect, and some of it would discourage those who may not be so committed to the ministry. Jesus reminds them of some of his previous teachings. Nothing happens in a vacuum in ministry. Everything is connected to everything else, and Jesus brings together many aspects of the ministry that these disciples had witnessed. He reminds them of what they have learned. A thorough pastor, Jesus has organized this particular group for this particular moment. This journey—and we don't know how long they were on their own apart from Jesus—was their trial run.

As he organizes this band of disciples for a "sent-out" ministry, Jesus does something that I would be hesitant to do. He gives them a lot more information than they seem to need for the journey. Sometimes we overload people with information, and they become discouraged. They will one day experience some of the things Jesus tells them, but not for several years. We know that they were successful in their two-by-two journey (e.g., Luke 9:6), but did they remember everything that Jesus taught them in preparation?

Luke 6:13 begins the choosing of the twelve from all the disciples who had been following Jesus. Jesus chooses the twelve and designates them as "apostles." It would be easy to gloss over this verse if not for the one that immediately precedes it. In verse 12, we read that Jesus had spent the previous night, the whole night, in prayer. Prayer is vital to the life of any faith-based organization. Too often, as pastors and congregants, we make decisions for which we do not seek God's guidance. There is sometimes an assumption that because we are the church, God will guide everything we do. I think this is a lie. I don't necessarily think we have to pray about things like what kind of cake to serve at the fellowship, but we should certainly go to God with decisions about our leadership, our mission, our ministry, and our worship. Jesus knew the importance of prayer for his organization and ministry, and any pastor worthy of the name should follow his example.

Every church is run by a group of people. Some are leaders by decision and vote, while others are leaders by charisma or the exercise of power apart from the decision of the whole. The larger body gives authority to both groups, either explicitly or implicitly. Jesus, as we see in John 15:16, chooses twelve people to be leaders. He clearly told them that he chose them—they did not choose him. They did not assert their authority or position to claim discipleship with Jesus. I have no doubt that there were times when some of them wished Jesus would have left them alone.

Why did Jesus choose these twelve men out of all those who followed him? Usually, the pastor is not the one to choose the lay leadership of the church, but Jesus did. Churches need some sort of criteria when choosing leadership. Because we don't know what criteria Jesus used in choosing the twelve, we have to devise our own list of qualifications. There are some areas in which we have to go in a different direction than Jesus did, but I think there are certain general principles we might apply from Jesus' choice of disciples. First of all, there are no children in the group, although some of the men were probably young. Second, he chose people from different socioeconomic strata. He also had no problems choosing relatives. I think the men Jesus chose were followers of the Law as they understood it. It seems that they were all Jews, although their community rejected some of them because of their occupation. None that we know of were leaders in their communities, although some, like John, seem to have had connections with local officials.

In addition to these, Jesus used the one criterion we can't use. Jesus knew their hearts. We can only discern the hearts—the sincerity, focus, desires, and passions—of those we consider as leaders in our churches. Jesus made good choices: although his disciples didn't seem to understand his message as he walked with them, when the time was right, because of his preparation and choices, only one of them was not able to go all the way with Jesus. Eleven out of twelve is a good percentage of staying power for volunteers.

Reflection Question

Are administration, efficiency, and stewardship vital parts of the ministry of the pastorate of your church?

Part Two

Jesus as Example of His Teachings

Jesus' life displays various aspects of the pastorate, as we explored in Part One. Now we will examine how Jesus demonstrates that he is an example of all his teachings. Jesus never taught anything that he did not live. Dr. S. D. Gordon wrote, "There are two ways of receiving instruction; one, by being told; the other, by watching someone else. The latter is the simpler and surer way."[1] Jesus was certainly a strong example to watch.

It does not take congregations long to discover if the pastor they have called is not true to the things that he or she preaches. It may be evident in conversations, in conflict situations, or in the everyday course of ministry. We all fall short—Jesus is the only perfect pastor. But when our lives demonstrate that our messages from the pulpit are only "sound bites," that they don't represent our lives, then a disjunction occurs in ministry. We are viewed as hypocrites who preach something that we aren't living.

One thing I have to do from time to time is offer the disclaimer that what I am preaching is something the Lord is working on in my life; it is not something I have received fully. Do we ever fully receive the teachings of our Lord? But it is one thing to know that God is working on something in our lives and another thing entirely to live in total contrast to what we preach.

Jesus lived everything that he taught for those who followed him. He enriched his teaching for them, and he still provides a wonderful example for us—an example of being an example. In this section, we will look at only a few of the teachings of Jesus that he lived, because he lived them all.

Note

[1]Lockyer, Herbert, *All the Prayers of the Bible* (Grand Rapids MI: Zondervan, 1959), 80.

1

Love

Mark 12:30-31; John 13:34; 14:21; 15:9

> *1 Corinthians 13:4-8*
> *Love is patient, love is kind. It does not envy, it does not boast, it is not proud. It is not rude, it is not self-seeking, it is not easily angered, it keeps no record of wrongs. Love does not delight in evil but rejoices with the truth. It always protects, always trusts, always hopes, always perseveres. Love never fails. . . .*

John 13:34 quotes Jesus as saying, "I give you a new commandment, that you love one another. Just as I have loved you, you also should love one another." The people Jesus ministered to knew the commandments—the Law was the source of their lives. God gave Moses ten of them, and the people quickly increased the number. By the time Jesus walked the earth, these original Ten Commandments had been multiplied into hundreds of laws that burdened the people with their vast numbers and the impossibility of actually keeping them all. Then Jesus came along and said that he had a new commandment. It wasn't a commandment to be added to all the others; it was a commandment to bring together the majority of the others. Jesus didn't come to do away with the Law but to fulfill it. Following this commandment would enable the people to fulfill the Law.

It is important to note that John 13:34 is one of two commandments Jesus gave. Mark 12:30-31 give us the full impact of Jesus' new commandment: "'. . . you shall love the Lord your God with all your heart, and with all your soul, and with all your mind, and with all your strength.' The second is this, 'You shall love your neighbor as yourself.' There is no other commandment greater than these."

Jesus demonstrated both of these commandments wholeheartedly. His entire life was committed to the Father. He spoke of this commitment, he spoke within it, and he lived it. Jesus never claimed any glory or honor for himself. He gave all glory and honor to the Father. If we do not first love God with all our being, our love for others will not be as it should be. The love of God must come first, but when we walk in that love, love for others will fall into place.

Jesus says that we are to love one another, and he demonstrated this kind of love in everything he did. When he spoke truthfully, although sometimes harshly, when he put his needs aside to minister to others, when he laid down his life for all humanity, and when he prepared twelve men to lead the church, he was leaving an example of love for us.

In John 14:21, Jesus demonstrates the fullness of love in our relationship to him and with the Father. Our love for Jesus is demonstrated by keeping his commandments, and this love is reciprocated by love from the Father and by love from the Son. God loves the world in general (John 3:16), but there is a different kind of love for those who demonstrate love by following Jesus.

In John 15:9, Jesus invites us to abide in his love. We need to learn the art of abiding. This doesn't mean that we follow Jesus when it is convenient for us, when it might suit our purposes, or only when we feel like it. To abide in Jesus' love can be understood by the way we abide in healthy, positive homes. We don't merely live there under sporadic conditions. Our homes are the places where we create families, where we have our meals, where we rest and recreate, where we learn and grow and spend the greatest amount of our time, under normal conditions. Our homes are where we learn how to interact with others, how we learn that we are not the center of the world, where we learn about God and faith and Christian witness. Abiding in Jesus' love can mean all the wonderful, positive things that abiding in our homes can mean. Abiding in Jesus is being in a place of growth and peace and, yes, love.

As Jesus' disciples walked with him, they learned to abide in his love. They knew that they were safe with him, they learned through their walk with him, and they grew as they put their trust in him. The disciples learned love as they walked with Jesus. They learned of the Father's love for them, which was different from what they may have been taught through the teachings of the Law, and they learned of Jesus' love for them. We know they learned, because they later demonstrated love for others.

Love should be the primary element of the church today. All that we do in our congregations should be based on love, not on rules or laws, traditions, or religion. We should base our actions on love for God and for one another. If we can get to that point, then we will truly be able to change the world.

Reflection Question

Do you love unconditionally?

2

Obedience

John 12:49; 14:15

> *Matthew 19:17*
> *"Why do you ask me about what is good?" Jesus replied. "There is only One who is good. If you want to enter life, obey the commandments."*

This is another word we don't like to hear too much today: obedience. The world has an attitude of "live and let live," which has penetrated the church. If it feels good, do it, no matter what the consequences may be. Don't worry about consequences; others can be made to take responsibility for them. Church discipline is hardly heard of these days, and I have no doubt that there are some who would not even be able to come up with an accurate understanding of what that means. We are encouraged to do what feels good and right, regardless of whether or not it is something we should do.

Jesus came in obedience to the will of the Father, and in doing so he set a remarkable example for us. In John 14:15,

Jesus teaches that love is shown through obedience, and that is what he lived. Jesus repeatedly reminds his hearers that he does nothing apart from the word of the Father. Perhaps the greatest example of Jesus' obedience is displayed in the garden of Gethsemane (Matt 26:39f). As he prays, he wants the cup of suffering, the cup of death, the cup of separation from the Father, to be removed from him. But, as strong as that desire is—and it was strong enough to cause him to sweat drops like blood (Luke 22:44)—his priority is the will of the Father. Jesus had demonstrated throughout his life that he lived for the will of the Father, and he wasn't going to change at the end of his earthly mission.

In John 12:49, Jesus provides the most succinct statement of his obedience to the Father: "for I have not spoken on my own, but the Father who sent me has himself given me a commandment about what to say and what to speak. And I know that his commandment is eternal life. What I speak, therefore, I speak just as the Father has told me."

It might be difficult, but we are able to follow this example. When our lives are submitted to the Holy Spirit, we should speak by the power and under the control of the Spirit. Jesus has given us commandments to love God first and then our neighbor, and the Spirit can certainly assist us in that. We demonstrate obedience to Jesus by the love we show others. We demonstrate our love for Jesus by our obedience. Whether we are speaking or acting, it should be a demonstration of obedience to our Lord and Savior.

Reflection Question

Why is it so important to be obedient to the Lord's teaching?

3

Childlike Faith

Mark 10:15

> *Matthew 18:4*
> *"Therefore, whoever humbles himself like this child is the greatest in the kingdom of heaven."*

Jesus taught that we must become like children to enter the kingdom (Mark 10:15). When we picture innocent little children, we think of trust, sincerity and openness, joy and laughter, wide-eyed amazement. We are to be strong in these qualities and weak in sophistication, worldliness, and knowledge.

How does Jesus set an example for us of being like a child? I think it is unfortunate that Scripture doesn't tell us that Jesus laughed. As he welcomed children, he certainly laughed with them. It is nearly impossible to be around young children for any length of time without laughing, although the innocence that often results in laughter seems to slip away quickly these days.

Children love to imitate their parents, and we can imagine Jesus doing this as a child. One commercial shows a father and son eating together, with the little boy doing everything the father does. And then, as an adult, John 5:19 relates Jesus saying that the Son only does what he sees the Father doing. As a faithful child, Jesus followed the examples set by the Father.

In the Ten Commandments, children are told to honor their fathers and mothers. Everything about Jesus' life honored his heavenly Father. Unfortunately, we are told little about Jesus' relationship with his earthly parents, especially his legal father, Joseph. He seems to honor his mother, but he begins the separation process early, knowing that he must stop being Mary's son and become the Child of the Kingdom. Therefore, he sometimes seems ungracious in his treatment of his mother. At age twelve, Jesus remained behind in Jerusalem after his parents started to return home from the Passover festival. When they returned to Jerusalem and found him, he honored their request that he return home with them, and he was submissive to them for the rest of his life in their home.

Jesus' final act of honoring of his mother was at the cross (which we studied in "Jesus as Caregiver"). He gave her as mother to the beloved disciple, and he gave that same disciple to Mary as her son. He thus spared her the life of a widow with no resources and made sure that she was welcomed into the home of one of his followers. His other siblings at that time were not believers in him, so Jesus probably wanted to make sure that his mother was included in the family of faith. While we know little of Jesus as a child, we can see by his adult behavior that he exercised the faith of a child in all of his endeavors. He was the child of his Heavenly Father, and he demonstrated his faith in the way he responded to his earthly parents and to all other people.

Reflection Question

What are the child-like qualities that make children so appealing as Kingdom candidates?

4

Servanthood

John 5:36

> *Matthew 20:26*
> *"...Instead, whoever wants to become great among you must be your servant."*

When we looked at Jesus as servant (ch. 12), we studied the prime example of his servanthood, the washing of the disciples' feet. He laid aside his authority, superiority, rights, and privilege to do the dirtiest, lowliest job of the lowliest servant.

How many of us are willing to put aside our rights and privileges to serve others? How many are willing to seek the highest good for others, regardless of how that may affect us? How many of us would be willing to die so that others might live? That is the example of servanthood Jesus leaves for us.

Jesus did great works as he walked the earth, but he never failed to say that he was doing the work of the Father

(John 5:36). Jesus could have had a fantastic following. He could have been the Messiah that so many people expected him to be. Instead, he had a commitment of servanthood—a determination to be servant to his Father first and then to all humanity.

In John 8:54, Jesus says, "If I glorify myself, my glory is nothing. It is my Father who glorifies me, he of whom you say, 'He is our God.'" A true servant never glorifies himself or boasts of accomplishments and possessions. A true servant gives glory to God for any praise received for his or her actions. A true servant knows true humility, not false modesty. Jesus demonstrates true humility.

Jesus also demonstrates the negative side of servanthood. People who serve others will be misunderstood. They will be taken for granted. I have friends who are afraid of being "doormats," but I have a hard time understanding how anyone could consider Jesus a doormat. True servants don't worry too much about people's responses. True servants seek the highest good for others, sometimes at great cost to themselves. This is the example Jesus leaves us, and it is an example well worth following.

Reflection Question

Are you a servant?

Part Three

Other Pastoral Factors of Jesus' Ministry

There are other factors of Jesus' ministry that can translate into ministry today. He had a congregation, he had detractors, and he even had pastor killers. Jesus ministered to outsiders as well as devoted followers. Jesus' needs were provided for. He was prepared for his ministry, and people had to cope with the effects of his absence. All of these things are part of the pastorate, and so we will look at each one.

1

Congregations

Luke 9:18; Matthew 4:25

Jesus ministered to two different sizes of congregation: very small and humongous. In Luke 9:18, we see him with his most common—and, I would daresay, favored—congregation: his disciples. While Jesus occasionally ministered to his "inner core," Peter, James, and John, for the most part he was with the Twelve, and that is what we see in this passage. Jesus is alone with his disciples.

There is a bit of contradiction here. We are told that Jesus was praying alone, with only his disciples near. Was he alone, or was he with his disciples? I think most pastors can solve this dichotomy. When we are leading worship, we are alone, except for God's presence, but we are also in the midst of the congregation. The people are present, and hopefully they are worshiping as we lead, but we are not physically together. We are not sitting with them but are often in a position elevated above them. The togetherness experienced at this time is spiritual, and I believe it was that way with Jesus and his disciples.

We are never told that Jesus' disciples prayed with him, so they could have been present while he prayed alone. This would have been a good example for them. When we pray, God, not other people, should be our focus. People might be the objects of our prayers, but God should always be our focus.

Following the prayer in Luke 9, Jesus raises a question with the disciples. I often like to introduce a sermon with a question for the congregation. After discussion of the question, Jesus begins his message. It is a message about himself. Faithful gospel messages always focus on Jesus. In this instance, Jesus tells his disciples about his upcoming passion. He then explains the necessity of self-denial and taking up the cross.

A sermon should always be easy for the congregation to understand. Jesus' little congregation certainly knew what crosses were, but did they understand the concept of taking up their cross? Had they seen convicts carrying their crosses? Did they realize that carrying a cross had a spiritual equivalent to the physical death Jesus would experience on the cross? Most pastors are unable to gauge the understanding of those who listen to them, but Jesus had an advantage in being able to discern the people's hearts.

Jesus also ministered to congregations of vast size, as we see in Matthew 4:25. As he journeyed between Galilee and Judea, and the land beyond (on the east side of) the Jordan, he drew large crowds. Jesus, because of who he is, is an exception to something I firmly believe: the pastor should never be the focus of the congregation. People came to see Jesus, and rightly so, but I don't think people should come to see pastors.

I have been in some mega congregations where the pastor or preacher was well known. He—and it is almost always a "he"—drew great crowds of people. Sometimes he had a faithful gospel message that pointed people to Jesus, and sometimes his message pointed people to himself or his particular ministry emphasis. When opportunities are presented to meet these pastors, I find that they often seem distant and unwelcoming. Maybe that is because of the burden of their ministry, but it is hard to see Jesus in such attitudes.

Jesus always seems to welcome the crowd. He even—or maybe specifically—welcomes "the least of these," the marginalized and the children. After preaching to one of his mega congregations, I can't imagine Jesus brushing off people who want to touch him or be near him. But there were times when he needed to get away. After feeding the five thousand, for example, he seems in a hurry to separate himself from the crowds and send his disciples off, so he can go and pray (Matt 14:22ff). I think there was a specific reason for this.

Whether we have large or small congregations, pastors need to take care of themselves physically, emotionally, and spiritually. When Jesus performed miracles, spiritual energy drained from him (e.g., Luke 8:46). In the Matthew passage, he had just performed an amazing miracle: multiplying five loaves of bread and two fish into enough food to feed five thousand people, with twelve baskets of leftovers (Mark 6:35-44). We can't always deny ourselves in order to meet the needs of our congregations. Jesus saw the need to go off and pray, to recharge, and he fulfilled that need. He didn't make apologies or excuses; he just ended the ministry, sent his disciples away, and went off to pray. He was exercising the self-care that all pastors should exercise. And then, after a season of prayer and refreshing, Jesus ministered once again to the crowds who sought him out.

Reflection Question

How important is the size of the congregation of which you are a part?

2

Outsiders

Matthew 15:22-28; 8:5-10

It was in an undergraduate religious studies class that I first heard the term "the other." I had been brought up in a home where I was taught to consider all people as equal, although I found out that this attitude was not always applied. Even though there was a period of decades between my life under my parents' roof and my undergraduate studies, that teaching never left me. So the idea of "the other" was a new concept for me. Why would we consider people as "other" from ourselves?

As a Jewish rabbi steeped in the Law of Moses, Jesus came to minister to the lost sheep of Israel, as we see in Matthew 15:22-28. It was forbidden for Jews to associate with Gentiles, whom they certainly considered "other." Jesus, however, was not so tightly bound to the tradition of his people that he refused to minister to those who came to him, even if they were outsiders in relationship to his religious foundations. He knew that they were never outsiders in the eyes of God.

The story of the Canaanite woman who comes to Jesus seeking relief and freedom for a demon-possessed daughter is a beautiful example of Jesus' ministry to outsiders. The Canaanites were kicked out of the land that God promised to his people (e.g., Deut 7:1). This woman was "marginalized" by her sex, her ethnicity, and perhaps her socioeconomic status. Jesus did not seek this woman out; she came looking for him.

Matthew tells us that she is not put off when reminded of Jesus' mission. Her faith has informed her that Jesus is the answer to her problem, and she will not give up. After Jesus tries to dissuade her—or possibly test her faith—with a statement about taking the children's (Israelites') food and throwing it to dogs (others), she is still not offended and refuses to go away. This outsider has a desire that compels her not to give up, and Jesus honors her faith by setting her daughter free from demon possession with just a word.

An even more remarkable story of Jesus' ministry to others is shown in Matthew 8:5-10. A high-placed Roman official comes to Jesus. This man is different in every way from the woman in the previous story, except that, like her, he is not Jewish and is thus also an outsider. He is a man of authority, a man who knows how to command people. But he can't command his servant to be well. Somehow he has heard of Jesus and his ability to heal. He humbles himself before Jesus and states his situation. When Jesus offers to go to his home (which would have offended Jesus' immediate congregation), the centurion protests and states his belief that Jesus can heal his servant right where he is, with just the right words. Amazed at this man's faith, Jesus complies with his requests.

In our pluralistic society, it is hard to think that any people could be considered "outsiders," especially within the church of Jesus Christ, and yet we can probably name plenty of examples. People who don't believe as we believe, who don't look like we look, and who do things that may not fit our personal approval profile are rejected in different ways. We may extend a cursory welcome to these people who visit us on Sunday, but somehow they rarely get included in social activities, never get invited to serve on a committee, and don't even get asked if they would like to join the church. The pastor must take the lead in such situations, just as Jesus did. His ministry to the "outsiders" gave powerful examples to his disciples. It took them a while to get the message, but, as we see in Acts, they ultimately followed his example and welcomed Gentiles into the new church.

Reflection Question

Do you know the "least of these" in your community? (See Matt. 25:40.)

3

Detractors

Matthew 9:34; 22:23-33; Mark 3:22

If a pastor has served in ministry for any length of time, it is truly remarkable if they have not encountered some type of resistance to an aspect of their ministry. I remember my first pastorate, which was an interim situation. The moderator informed me that all the church wanted was for me to preach the lectionary on Sunday and visit as necessary. As my ministry developed, I found that other people had different ideas, and even as an interim pastor, there were additional tasks that I was supposed to perform. As I began including other tasks in my ministry with that congregation, the tension between myself and the moderator grew.

Jesus, of course, had many detractors to his earthly ministry. The religious leaders were predominant among these. In Matthew 9:34 and Mark 3:22, Jesus is accused of performing his ministry by the power of Satan. If I were to receive such an accusation from a congregant, I think it would be time for me to start looking for other ministries. Jesus was not so dissuaded. People who knew the stories of their ancestry, having heard of the parting of the sea, the provision of manna, and the protection through the sojourn in the wilderness, should not have been put off by the wonders Jesus performed, but some of them were. They didn't relate Jesus to the God who had previously led their people.

Jesus didn't let such harsh criticism turn him away from his ministry. He went other places, where he continued proclaiming the gospel of the kingdom and curing every disease and sickness. Jesus had compassion for the people and a mission from the Father, and detractors wouldn't turn him away from either one.

Usually, Jesus' detractors were not as obvious in their disagreement with his ministry. The story of the Sadducees who asked Jesus the question about levirate law in Matthew 22:23-33 is a good example. The levirate law, set forth in Deuteronomy 25:5-10, called for a woman's brother-in-law to step into her husband's position if the husband died without producing offspring. We see an incident of this in Genesis 38:8-11.

It is hard to believe that the Sadducees were sincere in their questioning of Jesus. The little test they put before him was part of an ongoing plot to trap him. They created an imaginary scenario of a woman having seven brothers as husbands, one right after the other, with no offspring produced. Their inciting question was, "In the resurrection, whose wife of the seven will she be?"

Jesus' first clue to the insincerity of this group would have been their reference to the resurrection. Sadducees did not believe in resurrection. Jesus' response to this challenge may not be a good example of how a pastor should respond to congregational challenges! He insults these teachers of the law by telling them that they know neither the Scriptures nor the power of God. The people who witnessed the event were cheering Jesus on, but Jesus's response probably only increased the ire of this group of temple leaders.

Following the insult, however, Jesus gives a rational

answer, though we don't know if it stilled the waters. Jesus simply explained to them some of the aspects of resurrection life. First, people are neither married nor given in marriage in the resurrection (something a lot of our widows and widowers may not like hearing). Second, Jesus points out that the resurrection is provided by the God of the living, not the dead. Simple, truthful answers and a patient demeanor can often put an end to attempts at discrediting others.

Today, we have the Holy Spirit to guide us in handling our detractors. I remember a time when a couple took an actively antagonistic attitude toward me. They had been big supporters, but an announced position of mine set them against me. They began openly attacking me at every opportunity. This couple took part in many of the church's ministries and activities, and I couldn't avoid them, although all I wanted to do was run away from them. I sought God's guidance in this situation. God's answer was not gentle. In a short period, this couple experienced deaths in their family, both expected and unexpected. Rather than running away from them, I was drawn into closer ministry to them. As the season of sorrow passed, I could at least feel a little more comfortable in their presence, although we would never again know the supportive relationship we had once shared. And the issue that had severed our positive relationship never actually occurred, so their attitude and my concern were for nothing.

Jesus dealt with detractors in different ways, but he was always open to God's leadership through the Spirit, and so should pastors be today. Name-calling, revenge, spite, and other negative attitudes should never be part of our ministerial agenda or tool kit. Through God's Spirit, we have the power to turn detractors into supporters, if we will follow Jesus' example.

Reflection Questions

Can you identify the detractors to the ministry of your church? How do you respond to them?

4

Pastor Killers

Mark 10:33; 14:64

In reality, I think that "detractors" and "pastor killers" are two different types of people. In the church today, detractors may be those who are determined to show what they know or who may be driven by insecurities or fears. The latter may be people demonstrating extreme responses to fears and insecurities, or they may be people who are determined to control and willing to exercise that control in extreme ways. In Jesus' case, the detractors and the pastor killers were the same people. While there have been some examples of "pastorcide" in history, generally the term is metaphorical. In Jesus' case, of course, it was quite literal.

In Mark 10:33, Jesus knows that some people would welcome the first opportunity to end his ministry and his life. In truth, this is why Jesus came, but he could never convince his disciples of that. To some, it may seem that Jesus had a martyr complex, being determined to do things that would lead to his death. Jesus' mission, however, was not just about mission. He was fulfilling the will of the Father in reconciling all creation to God. The by-product of that mission is the salvation and forgiveness of sin made available for all humanity. The greatest gift in eternity was provided by Jesus' death, so it probably shouldn't be viewed as martyrdom.

Jesus' death would, however, have consequences similar to pastor killing. A particular ministry would end, although in Jesus' case, his ministry would be greatly expanded through the work of the Holy Spirit. Relationships would be changed or severed. Judas was never again part of the main group. The eleven who remained would not know Jesus according to the flesh, but they would be filled with and controlled by the Holy Spirit, sent by Jesus. Church life would change. It would no longer be about temple and synagogue worship. Groups would gather in homes and go forth to proclaim the gospel. Sometimes a pastor killing results in a split in the church. We see that happening in Acts as those who follow the Way separate from the synagogue and become a group totally distinct from Judaism. Although this separation was more gradual than most church splits, it had the same effect.

Some congregations seem to have a ministry in pastor killing. They may at first be excited about a new pastor coming, but they don't support their pastor. The pastor is given no authority beyond the pulpit, and what is said from the pulpit is often ignored. These congregations place demands on the pastor and the pastor's family that are unreasonable and sometimes impossible. They rarely participate in anything the pastor originates. They talk critically and negatively about the pastor wherever they go—and then they blame the pastor because they are not experiencing growth.

Consider the council meeting that took place on the night before Jesus' death, recorded in Mark 15. This meeting resembles many church meetings that have taken place. Jesus was brought before the council. Sometimes meetings are held without the pastor being present, and it seems likely that the council had made some prior provisions. After all, we are told that they were looking for testimony against Jesus so that they could put him to death. Their minds were already made up, and this is often the case with church meetings. The determination to end the pastorate had already been made.

We are told that many people gave false testimony against Jesus. Such might be the case in churches today, but I think it is more likely that people are repeating things they have heard without forming opinions of their own or looking deeper into the situation. Putting the pastor "on trial" is often the result of one or two discontented, influential people, "squeaky wheels," presenting their opinions and knowing that others will not stand against them. They give examples of the pastor's "misdeeds," like those who gave false testimony at Jesus' trial. Sometimes these accounts are given out of ignorance and sometimes out of pure spite, and they may or may not be true.

Having never attended a meeting like this, I don't know if pastors are given the opportunity to present their sides or not. It may depend on the governance of the church or the attitudes of the people. The constitution of the church I currently serve allows for calling a meeting but advises against saying what will happen at that meeting. Jesus was given an opportunity to present his case, but he was, at first, silent and did not answer the accusations. When he spoke, his words brought a cry of "blasphemy," and his fate was sealed.

Pastor-killing churches always put the blame on the pastor. They never seem to realize what they are doing, unless and until the Holy Spirit pays a visit and repentance happens.

In Jesus' case, the high priest, the elders, and the scribes never repent. They proceed with the actual execution, feeling that they have rid the world of a terrible nuisance, a threat to Judaism and the peace of Jerusalem. It is likely that many churches feel the same way when they have forced a pastor out of their pastorate and, sometimes, out of ministry altogether. Today, just as in Jesus' time, people do the things that seem right to them, regardless of the cost to others. Pastors should strive to consider all the costs before taking action, and they should guide their congregations to do the same.

Reflection Questions

Have you ever been a part of a pastor-killing experience?

How did it affect you?

5
Devoted Followers

Matthew 27:55-56; Mark 16:1, 9;
Luke 10:39, 42; John 20:11-17; 11:1-45; 12:1-8

As I have said before, I am not in favor of people becoming committed to their pastors, beyond the normal support and encouragement that is due the pastorate. Church shouldn't be about the pastor, but too often that seems to be the case. Some people take loyalty to their pastors to a place that the Lord never intended.

But some people just love their pastors, and Jesus had followers like that. All pastors should have at least a few of the kind of devoted followers that Jesus had.

In the past year, I underwent treatment for breast cancer. At various times, people sent cards, some brought food, and some simply could not do enough to support me. In Matthew 27:55-56, we are told of Jesus' supporters. These were probably financial supporters, people who provided food, lodging, and other expenses of Jesus' ministry, but any support is welcome. I know a retired pastor who has served a church as interim for ten years and collects no salary. The congregation he serves supports him in other ways, most specifically with gift cards to restaurants.

We think of Jesus being poor and without resources, but the Matthew text tells us that this was not the case. Because of the people—and they seemed to be mostly women—who supported him, he always had a place to stay, no matter where he was. He was never hungry unless he put himself intentionally in the way of hunger, as in fasting, and he didn't have to beg. Jesus and his followers had a "money bag" or common purse (John 12:6), and these supporters were probably contributing to the coins in that purse. Jesus and his disciples never went without—unless that was the point of a mission on which Jesus sent them—and they had money to give to the poor (John 12:5). (See more about this kind of support under "Provision" in this section.)

Today, we support our pastors indirectly by supporting the ministry of the church. Support of the church budget provides the salary and other benefits to the pastor, as well as providing for various ministries and educational opportunities. God doesn't need our money. Our giving shows our love for the Lord and the Lord's work. To the extent that we have received God's love in our life, so we will give for God's work in the lives of others.

Two women exemplify the support shown to their pastor Jesus. These women may or may not have contributed to Jesus' financial support, but both were devoted followers. One is Mary Magdalene, and the other is Mary, the sister of Martha and Lazarus.

While we are not told the specific circumstances of Jesus' first encounter with Mary of Magdala, we know that he set her free from the possession of seven demons (Luke 8:2; Mark 16:9). Since the number seven is a perfect, complete number, we might conclude that her possession was complete and thorough. Her devotion to Jesus following her deliverance certainly was. There is no one more devoted to Jesus than Mary Magdalene. We don't hear much about her until Jesus' passion, but from the cross to the grave, she is present. In most cases, we see her with other women. An exception is John's resurrection story. With some reference to the presence of others, John presents Mary Magdalene alone at the tomb on resurrection day, tearful and searching (John 20:1ff). When she first discovered the removal of the stone, she ran to tell others. When they had come, investigated, and left, she remained, still seeking. Her perseverance paid off when she encountered Jesus. This devoted, formerly demon-possessed woman became the first witness to the resurrected Christ, and she was given the first mission of the gospel of resurrection: to go and tell others, thus making her the first evangelist of the resurrection. What a privilege and a reward for one who had lived in an attitude of gratitude for what her pastor had done for her.

Mary of Bethany, the sister of Martha and Lazarus, appears devoted to Jesus, but we are not told why. Her attitude toward Jesus is demonstrated in ways that go beyond the norm for appreciation of a pastor and that would today, as in her day, be considered scandalous. Her love for Jesus, however, cannot be denied.

We first meet Mary in what seems to be the home of her sister, Martha (Luke 10:39ff). Martha has invited Jesus and his friends for dinner. As one desiring to demonstrate loving hospitality, Martha is busy with the kitchen work. She probably expects that Mary will be also. But where is Mary? She is in with the men, sitting at Jesus' feet, listening. I can relate to that in a way. As a youngster and young woman, I rarely wanted to do what the women were doing. I was interested in sports, and it wasn't usually the women who discussed the most recent game.

Martha is disgruntled that she is not receiving the expected help, and she complains to her pastor, Jesus. She wants him to make her sister help her in the kitchen. Most pastors, of course, don't get involved in kitchen responsibilities, and Jesus didn't either. He actually rebuffs Martha, telling her that Mary, by sitting and listening to him, had chosen the best thing. Listening to Jesus is more important than preparing a meal. Many will protest that the work has to be done, but that isn't what Jesus says. If we have a choice between Bible study and fellowship, the former should take priority. Hopefully, we can enjoy both within our congregations.

We next meet Mary following her brother Lazarus's death (John 11:1-45). Mary is not the first one to greet Jesus as he comes to minister to the bereaved sisters. Martha is. The sisters say the exact same words, but with different attitudes. Martha might be seen as scolding Jesus when she says, "if you had been here, my brother would not have died," although she does seem to make a profession of faith in Jesus' ability to change the situation. Mary approaches Jesus with tears and by kneeling at his feet, both absent from Martha's approach. Mary repeats the words of Martha, but there is not the discourse between the two of them that took place between Jesus and Martha as Jesus tried to get Martha to understand that he is the resurrection. Mary seems to know this already, and her response to his presence causes Jesus' own tears.

Our final visit with Mary is the scandalous one in John 12:1-8 (also see Matt 26:6-12; Mark 14:3-9). This Scripture leads me to believe that something happened between Mary and Jesus of which we are not told. It may have been a healing, maybe a deliverance from demon possession, maybe the forgiveness of some particular sin—I don't know—but such devotion usually has a foundation beneath it. Again, Mary is with the men rather than helping in the kitchen, but this time her actions are more pronounced. She is not passively sitting; she has acquired a precious ointment and is putting it on Jesus' feet and wiping them with her hair. The disciples with Jesus—and John mentions Judas specifically—are outraged that this ointment was not sold and the money given to the poor. Jesus, the pastor, quiets their complaints, but probably not their discontent, by saying that Mary has provided this anointing for his burial. Jesus again affirms that which others find out of place.

(There is a similar story in Luke about a sinful woman who comes into a dinner party and anoints Jesus with tears and ointment, but there are too many differences in the story to believe that the upright, Jewish Mary of Bethany is the sinful woman of the unknown place in Luke 7:37-48.)

We have seen, in my lifetime, pastors who allowed their congregations to become too devoted to them. Jim Jones and David Koresh are only two examples. While Jesus always encourages us to follow him, he would never have permitted such fanatic attachment. This is demonstrated in his entry into Jerusalem. The people wanted to make him king, and he is indeed a King, but not the kind of militaristic king the people wanted. Jesus had the strength and commitment to resist the needs and desires of the people that conflicted with his mission. Unhealthy attachment to a pastor is often the fault of pastors who lose sight of the reason they are called to serve and the fault of the people who blindly follow such pastors. The more closely we walk with the Lord, the less likely we are to develop inappropriate attachments.

Reflection Question

How can pastors avoid having congregants attach themselves too closely to the pastor?

6

Preparation

Luke 2:41-52; Matthew 3:13-17; 4:1-11

Jesus had a ministry of preparation. He spent many hours preparing his disciples for the time when they would lead the church. He prepared them by word and deed. He prepared them for the time when he would no longer be at their side, guiding them in their discussions and decisions. Jesus was a great preparer, but how much thought do we give to the preparation that Jesus underwent for his own ministry?

It is easy to think that, because of his relationship to the Father, Jesus came to earth fully prepared for his ministry. No pastor on earth has ever been fully prepared for his or her ministry from birth, and we should not expect that Jesus was. It is true that Jesus entered his earthly life with a mission, but he had to spend time in preparation for that mission.

Jesus' preparation began in childhood. We know little about Jesus' childhood, but I think we can assume that regular synagogue attendance and study of the Scriptures were part of his early years. I don't think Jesus came downloaded with full knowledge of all the Scriptures. His parents regularly took him to Jerusalem with them for the required festivals. We have one account of such faithfulness in Luke 2:41-52.

Jesus and his parents would not have traveled alone. They likely made the trip with other family members and friends. That is one of the reasons Jesus' parents didn't immediately notice his absence. In a large family group, all the adults took care of the younger members. Children traveled with the women. Since Jesus was twelve, on the verge of adulthood, the women might have assumed that he was traveling with the men. So a full day passed before they noticed his absence, and it was three days before they found him in the temple.

Jesus was found with the teachers in the temple, listening and asking questions. Often when I am in a group, I am reluctant to ask questions because I often don't understand enough to ask. Jesus must have understood enough to ask questions. We are told that those present were amazed at his understanding and his answers. This was not a natural phenomenon. Jesus had probably studied the Scriptures from early childhood, first by hearing and then by his own personal study. When he made this trip to the temple, he had many years of preparation behind him. His parents must have been involved in this preparation, and yet they seem confused by his behavior.

When Jesus' mother questions his presence there, rather than with the traveling family, Jesus clearly doesn't understand her concern. She and Joseph have helped to prepare him for this day. They have surely assisted with his study of the Scriptures. They must have been instrumental in seeing that he attended synagogue. Why, then, are they surprised that he is now beginning to break into the activity for which he has been prepared?

Beyond the things Mary and Joseph may have done during Jesus' childhood, they should have had memories of the circumstances of his birth. An angel had appeared to Mary to proclaim his pending birth. The conception was miraculous. Angels proclaimed his birth to shepherds in the field. Wise men traveled long distances to visit the young child. Why can't his parents understand when he explains that he has to be in his Father's house?

For Jesus, this incident opened the door into ministry, although he did not remain in Jerusalem. He likely could have stayed and studied under one of the rabbis. We are told, however, that he returned home with his parents and was submissive to them.

Not all pastors begin their preparation in early childhood. I was well into middle adulthood when I was called to the pastorate, although I can look back and point to various steps of preparation throughout my life. I know many pastors who received early calls to ministry and began some preparation, if only by coming under the mentorship of their pastors. Blessed are the pastors who recognize a call or potential call in one of their congregants and take that young person under their wing in preparation for the call God might bring into that life.

I wonder if Jesus had a mentor in Nazareth. Did some rabbi take him under his wing and give him special training in Scriptures? Did one of the leaders of the synagogue see the potential in the child Jesus and encourage him in his studies? It seems unlikely that Jesus arrived at the temple that day without someone having contributed to his preparation for this public appearance as a scholar of the Scriptures.

Preparation in and knowledge of Scriptures are not the only pastoral qualities we see in Jesus in this account. The fact that he was submissive to his parents is important. Pastors too need to learn submission. Pastors are not independent contractors. They first must be submissive to God, who has given them their calling and gifts for ministry. Then, they must be submissive to the congregation who has called them to ministry. While pastors may be the leaders of God's church, they can't be independent. Submission to the authority of the congregation is the outcome of their submission to God.

Once Jesus reached adulthood and began his ministry, we see another step of preparation: his baptism (Matt 3:13-17).

For most of us, baptism is an early step of faith that brings us into the family of God. One's call to the pastorate would usually follow baptism, but not always. Sometimes the call comes first. For Jesus, the call to ministry came long before his baptism, and his baptism came later as he prepared to begin the ministry ordained by the Father.

Why was Jesus baptized? He tells John the Baptizer that it is to be done to "fulfill all righteousness" (Matt 3:15). Jesus intentionally goes to John to be baptized. John recognizes that he is not worthy and indeed that Jesus should be baptizing him. John certainly does not treat Jesus as he treated the sinners who had come for baptism. John submits to Jesus' assertion that his baptism is part of God's will for Jesus.

As he undergoes baptism, Jesus sets an example not only for his disciples but also for pastors. He does not hold himself above others. Instead, he joins in the ritual of those who needed cleansing from their sin, thus identifying with the people to whom he would minister. He sets the example of doing what is pleasing to God, which should always be the goal of the pastor.

As Jesus comes up out of the water, the heavens are opened, the Holy Spirit in the form of a dove lands on him, and a voice from heaven proclaims God's pleasure with his beloved Son. What a wonderful commission for ministry!

And Jesus still has one more stage of preparation. As soon as Jesus is baptized, he is led by the Spirit into the wilderness, according to Matthew 4:1-11. His preparation for ministry continues. Jesus does not journey into the wilderness on his own. Matthew and Luke are gentle in their description of Jesus' compulsion. Mark is not so gentle, saying that the Spirit "sent him out" (NIV) or "impelled him to go" (NAS). The King James is even more explicit: the Spirit "driveth him" into the wilderness. Jesus goes neither under his own will nor under his own power.

The first thing Jesus does is fast for forty days and forty nights. I have found fasting to be a great preparation for any situation I am about to face. Fasting helps me submit my flesh to my spirit. The time spent not eating should be a basis for time spent with the Lord. Through prayer and meditation on Scripture, I believe that we can draw on God's strength to help us face whatever comes.

Did Jesus know what awaited him following his time of fasting? We aren't sure, but, as Satan began his temptation, Jesus was ready. I think the enemy may have thought that fasting would put Jesus in a weakened condition, and, physically, that may have been the case. But it was not the case spiritually and emotionally. The tempter's work had a spiritual foundation, but it appealed to material and real interests.

Jesus faces three tests of the tempter. The first is to provide nourishment for himself, a reasonable desire after forty days of fasting. This is the temptation for physical desires. If Jesus can turn stones to bread, he can change any source into whatever he desires. But Jesus hasn't come to satisfy his own desires. One day, he will provide bread for others, but he won't do so for his personal needs and desires. Jesus rejects Satan's temptation by quoting Deuteronomy 8:3. His preparation in the Scriptures will continue to serve him well during this time of testing.

The next test seems to be a test of the desire for fame and popularity. A person jumping from a pinnacle of the temple would draw a lot of attention. Think how the people would talk about Jesus if the angels come to rescue him from harm. The people would certainly be willing to follow such a person. Jesus will indeed collect a group of followers in his ministry, but he will do so through works that honor God, not the enemy of God.

This temptation would also show how beloved Jesus is of God. Jesus has already had that affirmation at his baptism; he doesn't need to get it through spurious means. Jesus possibly draws his scriptural response from Deuteronomy 6:16, but it could come from a number of other Scriptures.

The enemy's final test is the temptation for power. Who wouldn't want to own the whole world? But at what cost? Many people have, in a sense, sold their souls to Satan for much less. The tempter doesn't seem to know that, if Jesus fulfills his mission, he will have all things put under him anyway (John 13:3; Rom 11:36). Again, he will one day gain what Satan offers, but he will get it in a way that glorifies the One who sent him, not in a way that satisfies the desires of his flesh, if he had such desires. Jesus' scriptural response is part of the Law he has known all his life: Deuteronomy 6:13-14.

As pastors prepare for ministry, whether formally or informally, it is important that their preparation honors God. Some believe that Jesus could not have given into the temptations placed before him. I believe he could have; otherwise, there is nothing to prove in having him go through those temptations. Jesus' entire agenda was to honor the Father, and he accomplished this at every turn. He faithfully studied the Scriptures, he fulfilled the righteousness of baptism, and he was able to overcome the strong temptations placed before him by the enemy. Jesus was ready to begin his ministry.

Reflection Question

What is the minimum preparation you believe a minister should have for the pastorate?

7

Provision

Matthew 27:55; Mark 15:40-41;
Luke 8:3; 2 Chronicles 31:5-9

As my husband graduated from seminary, I was called to return there. I didn't understand why. It was a clear message upon my heart, and I had to follow it, but I had some preparation to do. I still had to obtain an undergraduate degree. Wonderful doors opened up to enable me to get that degree, and I graduated with highest honors. In the spring before I planned to start at seminary, I was told that a scholarship I had previously been promised would not be available. We saved the money necessary to get me through my first semester, but I had no idea where any additional funds would come from. I thought it would be one and done. During the first week of my first semester at seminary, however, a relative passed away, leaving my husband and me with enough funds to assure that I would be able to complete seminary.

When the Lord calls us to a ministry, the Lord provides for that ministry. When I was at seminary, I had no idea that the pastorate was on the horizon for me; I had planned to go to a Jewish school to get a Ph.D. in Hebrew and Old Testament background.

From the outset, Jesus was certain of the ministry he would have until the fulfillment of his mission on Calvary. The Father was faithful throughout to make sure that he had all he needed to fulfill his ministry along the way.

I recently had a discussion with some folks who insisted that women did not travel with Jesus. Matthew 27:55 assures us that they did. There were women at the cross in Judea, and these women had followed Jesus from Galilee to minister to his needs. This is a distance of about 135 miles, as the crow flies, but it was not gentle terrain. The women made this trip (or trips) to assist Jesus—and, I am sure, the men with him—with cooking, perhaps sewing, and other areas of ministry they could perform. I see Jesus as the pastor for these women as they traveled. I have no doubt that one of these women was his mother, perhaps serving as a chaperone.

Although Mark says that "many" women came up to Jerusalem with Jesus, he gives us the names of two of these women (15:40-41): Mary Magdalene and another Mary who is identified as being the mother of James, Joses, and Salome. I happen to believe that this is one of the ways Jesus' mother was identified after he handed her into the care of John (John 19:27) from the cross: as "Mary, mother of . . . ." She became John's mother at the cross, no longer the mother of Jesus. In Acts 1:14, Mary is identified as the mother of Jesus. That is the only place, following the crucifixion, where she is so identified. It is inconceivable that she would not have been at the cross or at the tomb. I believe that she was there but is identified in other ways, including "the other Mary" of Matthew 27:61 and Matthew 28:1.

Whoever these women are that Mark lists, they came up with Jesus to Judea and had ministered to him as far away as Galilee. I think most of these women came from Galilee. Mary Magdalene was from Magdala, which was in Galilee. Jesus' mother would have been from Nazareth, which was in Galilee. And some women could have joined along the way. Perhaps the woman at the well in Sychar was among the many women whom Mark mentions. These women gave of their resources to assist Jesus' ministry, thus engaging in their own ministries.

Luke tells us that it wasn't just ordinary women who ministered to Jesus. In 8:3, we are told that Joanna, the wife of a member of King Herod's court, ministered to him of her substance. We are never given a total count of all the women who ministered to Jesus, but they were apparently abundant and generous.

Many questions might be raised as to how women were able to support the ministry of Jesus. Some could have inherited from families. Some could have traded in land and livestock and made a nice living. Perhaps some had generous allowances from their husbands. In Bethany, a woman named Martha opened "her" home to him. Women were able to accumulate and use wealth.

The generosity of the people of Israel is well documented. Perhaps 2 Chronicles 31:5-9 gives us the most specific example of this generosity. During a time of revival, Israel poured out their abundance for their priests and Levites so that they could do the work of ministry and their families would be provided for. The people responded to a call to care for their religious leaders with an abundance of all good things, including a tithe of everything. The gifts piled up in heaps. The priests and Levites had all they needed, and the heaps were the leftovers.

Churches that support their own pastors follow this model. The pastor is not hired but called. The money received by the pastor provides for the pastor's family as the pastor does the work of ministry. The women who followed and ministered to Jesus did so in order that he could do the work of his ministry as he traveled the land. He was faithfully committed to the ministry to which he was called, and the Father provided for his needs. The Father will also provide for the pastor's needs today.

Reflection Question

Besides salary and standard pastoral expenses, in what ways does your congregation provide for their pastor?

8

Aftermath

John 20:11-28; 21:15-24; Acts 1:6-11; 2

All pastorates eventually come to an end, whether by death, retirement, a new calling, or discord between congregation and pastor. Jesus' earthly pastorate came to an end in a way that few pastors experience, but it was neither unplanned nor avoidable. The cross was the culmination of all Jesus had done as he sojourned on earth.

The crucifixion was a horrible blow to Jesus' congregation. The disciples fled. The women remained, looking on from afar, likely with tears blurring their vision. I am sure the emotions could be compared to those of a congregation suddenly losing their pastor to death. Shock, fear, and confusion prevail. Questions about the future, about survival, about immediate needs would abound.

Churches today don't get to experience the resurrection of their pastor, as Jesus' congregation did. Sorrow and fear were replaced, sometimes suddenly, sometimes gradually, with surprise and joy. They got to spend time with their beloved pastor once again, and Jesus' pastoral ministry continued in these times.

Mary Magdalene went to the tomb to continue her ministry to her pastor, but she found the tomb empty and got another dose of sorrow. Then, as she waited outside the tomb, her Shepherd appeared to her. He spoke her name, and she recognized him. Always the pastor, he enabled her to engage in a new ministry: telling the good news of his resurrection. Mary, as mentioned earlier, became the first evangelist of the Risen Lord, and Jesus continued his ministry of preparation.

One of my favorite post-resurrection stories is the story of Jesus and the breakfast on the beach in John 21:15-24. (I discussed this passage in "Jesus as Enabler/Preparer.") In a brilliant example of pastoral ministry, Jesus brings healing to Peter's heart, reinforcing his value to the kingdom of God and further preparing him for his own ministry.

Jesus continued his pastoral ministry immediately prior to his ascension and return to the Father. As he gathered with his disciples (Acts 1:6-11), they asked about what was to come. Jesus told them that was not their concern. They must be about their new job: being the witnesses of Jesus and the kingdom in their immediate area and throughout the world. And of course, as a faithful pastor, Jesus let them know that they would not be alone. God's Spirit would empower them for this ministry. Then Jesus was taken up into the heavens right before their eyes, renewing their sorrow. But they were not to continue in sorrow. Jesus dispatched two angels to comfort them and let them know that Jesus would return in the same way they had seen him depart. The disciples expected this to happen immediately, but soon, there would be other things to occupy their thoughts and replace their sorrow.

Good pastors keep the promises they make, and Jesus was no exception. He had promised his followers a Comforter or Counselor, the Spirit of truth (John 15:26). That spiritual guidance arrived during the first festival of Pentecost following Jesus' ascension (Acts 2). As 120 disciples, male and female, waited to see how Jesus' promise would be fulfilled, the Spirit fell upon them, changed their lives, and helped them give birth to an organization that had never been seen on the face of the earth, before or since. Many of these people, who had followed Jesus during his pastoral ministry, were about to engage in their own pastoral ministry, empowered by the Spirit who had accompanied Jesus. They had been prepared and taught by the best. Now, the fruit of Jesus' pastoral ministry was about to burst forth in full bloom. This fruit is still being developed and shared today.

Reflection Question

How do you believe a pastor can prepare a congregation for his or her departure?

CPSIA information can be obtained at www.ICGtesting.com
Printed in the USA
BVOW11s1755160614

356467BV00005B/18/P

9 781938 514586